Cornbread in Heaven

Crumbs and Pieces of a Sweet/Savory Life

JULIE G. OLMSTED

Cornbread in Heaven

Copyright © 2025 by Julie G. Olmsted

All rights reserved.

Published by Red Penguin Books

Bellerose Village, New York

ISBN

Digital 978-1-63777-810-4

Print 978-1-63777-811-1

No part of this book may be reproduced in any form or by any electronic or mechanical means, including information storage and retrieval systems, without written permission from the author, except for the use of brief quotations in a book review.

Contents

Introduction	vii
The Shattering	1
Life Without Him	4
Oklahoma Roots	8
On the Skids	11
Surprising Meanness	14
Daddies, Various	16
A Daughter's Reflection	19
Hillbilly Diet	22
The Widening Circle	24
Unhinged	28
Chickens and Church	31
Dreams, Various	36
Up, Down - Together, Apart	38
New Worlds	46
Opal	49
Happy and Gay	51
Pulling Away	53
Leaving Again	57
Wheels of Fun	58
Those Lucky People	60
Work as a Refuge	65
Boys and Booze	68
Leaving for Good	72
An Education of Sorts	75
Herm	80
A Crack Appears	82
Den	88
Kansas City	93
Michael	96
Crossing the Rubicon	98
Speeding Up	101
Slowing Down	104
Exploring the Vast Unknown	106

A Personal Myth	111
Transformation	112
Starry Sky	115
Cornbread in Heaven	116
Vegas	122
Oklahoma City	125
Dallas	127
New York at Last	129
Rick	136
Unlikely Help	137
Last Stop	140
Ticket to Ride	143
Afterword	149
Acknowledgments	151

To My Mother and My Children

Introduction

Washing dishes at the sink is a solitary act that brings me some peace, especially at night. I can access interrupted thought fragments from the day, re-think misunderstandings, reflect on the mundane and the profound. When the small, overhead light shines on the water and the bubbles, I see my hands, now so much like my mother's, veins once obscured by the smoothness of youth, now prominent. I see the strength, the years, the endless chores. The flurry of her fingers, intent on any task, like stirring a soup, mopping a floor or patching a pair of pants. Washing dishes, "tidying up," cleaning out the car or any number of other tasks remind me of scenes of the past and make me see how my daily ordinary movements trace the same patterns as my mother's. I wonder, *are all these tasks, tasks that really need to be done? Or an avoidance of tasks that call softly in less obvious ways?* Tasks like writing a poem, playing the piano, or reading a book. Mom never stopped tending, cleaning, striving for something. Approval? Release? Perfection? Permission to just be? Or was it that she was trained, like me, from an early age in the blue collar way of "work till you drop?"

Now after hundreds of jobs which include waitress and busser, secretary, factory worker, receptionist, housecleaner, meatpacker, English teacher, night club singer, Weight Watcher leader, social worker, housewife and mother, I am putting the finishing touches on over thirty years of ministry. Unlikely yet entirely predictable, when you consider the surprising work of Spirit and the religion of my parents and grandparents. All those jobs, and day after day, there are always the dishes.

One night recently, I rinsed the last one, wiped down the counter, then opened the back door to head outside to the small deck off the back of the house. The sky is my ever-present confidante and comforter. Holding myself and breathing in the slightly chilly air, I set my gaze on the sprinkling of stars I could see through the trees and listened to the blessed sounds of fading summer, crickets, toads, mysterious birds, a distant dog barking. I listened and said to my friend the sky, *Maybe I will try to write down these memories that float up like bubbles.* These stories I hold in my heart, so much like my mother's, which more and more, seem to be one. Mom's life was tumultuous, filled with obstacles and dead ends. I dedicate this effort to capture our lives in words to her.

In thought, I see us in our waitress uniforms, having done our best to

Introduction

make ourselves presentable, hiding any flaws or blemishes in our faces or figures, with aprons, makeup, good grooming and a bit of flair here and there, like earrings, a scarf, a pin, some glitter on the hair or eyelids. I can feel the anticipation of an evening out on the town. Who would we meet? How would the night end? Would life dish up something surprising and wonderful just before going home? I see us driving up and down the Ozark hills, singing and planning, just where would we stop and have lunch? I hold both of us now in this "after-youth-life" with tenderness, and happiness for the present moment. Looking up from my spot on the deck, breathing in and out, treasuring the sounds of hidden life around me, I wince with some embarrassment at our long-gone youth, yet gratitude fills me, mixed with acceptance of loss and time passing.

These are the times of trial and longing. These are the scenes of wrong turns and right action for return to gentler paths. These are the rocky, thorny, sandy, muddy searches for a kind of peace that lasts a while. I was listening to many voices in those years, many inner arguments with myself, and a steady chorus of, "Not this, not this. Oh no, not this." And of course, music. What were the songs of the day that infused my travels? We'll Sing in the Sunshine, Like a Rolling Stone, Ticket to Ride, San Francisco, California Dreamin'…, Love Train. My childhood home could not hold me. I loved it, held it inside me, and had to leave it. The leaving was in my soul. As for so many others, I had to get away. Many loves, a thousand cuts to the heart, and, honestly, a fractured mind, that had to be blown and come back together in its own time. Somehow.

THE SHATTERING

Invisible Me

It was my third birthday. I knew about birthdays by now: the years, the cake, the gifts. When asked how old I was, I held up my fingers shyly. Daddy moved out a while ago. Mommy said it was her best friend, Marge. Daddy said mom was just too much. I didn't understand what he meant but thought better of asking any questions about it. I think I didn't want to know. At night the three of us slept together in one bed. That is, Sissy slept. Mommy cried. I tried to comfort her. Her sadness was heavy and bewildering. *What could I do*, I always thought. I would end up patting her shoulder with my small hand, "Okay, Mommy. It's okay." Night after night, the sobbing.

"How far is heaven?" came the song by Kitty Wells and her daughter from the radio. Let's go tonight… I knew Daddy wasn't in heaven, but the song made tears in my eyes. I want my daddy, too, I thought. Once, he took me away for a night. We slept in his small, rented room. There were bunk beds and I got to sleep on the top. Outside the window pretty neon lights flashed off and on, off and on. G-I-R-L-S. F-O-O-D, F-U-N. Daddy seemed sad, too. I didn't understand. I watched as my handsome daddy moved about the room. I fell asleep and, in the morning, we had pancakes. We all, Mommy, Sissy, and I, wanted Daddy to come back.

But now, it was my birthday, and everything would be fine because it was special. To me, August 1st was the best day of the year. Everything is green and warm. There is sunshine, swimming and lemonade, trees in bloom, and sweet-smelling flowers everywhere. My birthday was the best day of all. There will be happy times no matter what on that day.

Daddy came to the door but not into the house. Mommy and I were behind the screen door. The sun was shining through the screen from the front porch. Daddy stood there, hands in his pockets. He wore a gray khaki shirt and pants from his work at the body shop. Emery, I read on the shirt pocket. That meant he was important, very special, like my birthday. Why was he not smiling? I was small and he and Mommy were big. It seemed like they didn't see me. It's my birthday! I wanted to scream. I couldn't understand. Can't you see me standing here? Where's my smile, my hug, my presents, my cake? I wanted my Daddy to hold me tight. Daddy didn't look at me. I felt invisible.

Julie G. Olmsted

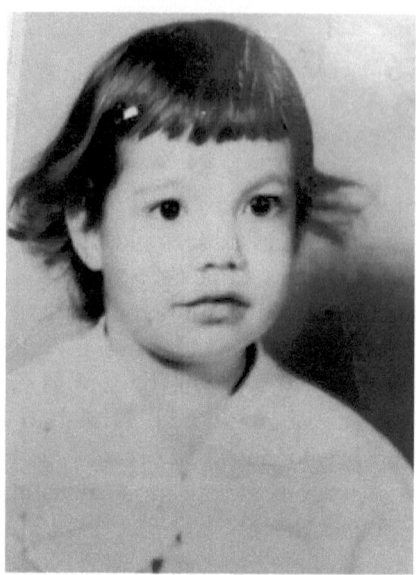

Baby Girl - Serious Already, Age 2

My mom was pretty. She wore a navy-blue dress with white polka dots. She stood there, beautiful, and young, with wavy brown hair and white, shiny teeth. She was a lady. But the lady was angry. Something about his car. She said she hated his car, a red and white brand-new Buick. She hated his car because he loved his car more than he loved her. And there is her friend Margie. Margie who was skinny next to Mommy. Margie who wore short shorts and high heels. Margie, with tight sweaters and perfect make-up. She used a powder puff to wipe her butt. That's what Mommy said. Once, after they were married and I visited, I checked. I told Mommy it wasn't true. She used toilet paper like everyone else. Mommy laughed, hugged me, then cried.

Daddy said he couldn't come in even though Mommy begged. "Come in for cake, at least," she said. Can't do it," said Daddy. *Where's my hug?* I kept thinking. But I said nothing because I was invisible. Their voices kept getting louder and louder. Daddy turned to go. No! You can't go now. It's my birthday. But I never said the words. Because I was invisible. Daddy turned to step off the porch and out to his car. Where did the knife come from? It was huge, a butcher knife; that's what everyone called it. We heard the words butcher knife a lot. Butcher knife. Ball peen hammer. Razor strap. A razor strap hung on the back door. Sissy and I thought it would be used on us if we didn't behave. "I'll get after you with the razor strap," Mom would sometimes say. And we hurried to do what we were supposed to.

Mom raised the butcher knife and was screaming at Daddy. She stepped out onto the porch and threw it his way as hard as she could. Is this what Daddy meant when he said that Mommy was just too much? Daddy said she threw the knife at him and tried to kill him. Mom said she threw it at his stupid car.

Life Without Him

We moved to a house on Pleasant Street in Aurora. It was half a house, with a big living room. Other people lived on the other side of the house, and I learned that was called a duplex. Our dog Rowdy had brown and white curly hair and huge brown eyes. He was almost as big as me. Back and forth through the big living room we ran, again and again. I played outside on the sidewalk with my Cinderella doll and stroller. Our babysitter was Martha O'Dell, tired and skinny, with long stringy hair. Mom said she put dirty clothes into dresser drawers. The razor strap hung on the door in the back room. It didn't get used, but we always knew it was there. Martha O'Dell talked about the razor strap, too. "I'll get that razor strap after you!" Sissy and I behaved.

We had two old couches, back-to-back. Mom slept on one, me on the other. At night when she came home from work, we would hold hands across the couches till I fell asleep. Sissy slept in the bedroom. I worried about mom because she worked so hard. She would tell me her feet hurt and I would rub them with rubbing alcohol.

"Mommy, don't let go of my hand.'

"I won't, sweetie."

"I love you, Mommy."

"I love you, too, baby. With all my heart."

I love my daddy, too. I say a prayer, "God bless Mommy and Daddy." They are together in my prayer.

Santy Claus came while I was sleeping one night. He tiptoed around, putting presents under the tree. Santy Claus had black hair and a white beard. The tree lights were blinking off and on, and Santy made no sound. I was so happy to see him! But I was careful to not open my eyes much. I didn't want Santy to see my eyes open. I know Santy sees me when I'm sleeping. Being good was very, very important, not just to avoid the razor strap, but to get good stuff anytime, including Christmas!

Mom always had to look good to go to work as a waitress. She taught me to polish her shoes. "Polish my shoes, baby." "Okay, Mommy." "Did I do a good job?" "Yes, sweetie, you did a very good job." The white swab came out of the bottle. The shoes were on newspaper to protect the floor.

Life Without Him

I swabbed carefully, making sure there wasn't too much or too little on the swab. When they were dry, I used a rag to shine them up. Mom washed the shoelaces along with her nylons and girdle. Everything looked spick 'n span.

She took a bath every morning. There wasn't a shower, and I never took one until I went to college. I could hear Mom splashing water, washing with Ivory soap, then calling me in to wash her back. "Oh, that feels so good, honey. Thank you so very much." "You're welcome, Mommy." Back to bed.

She almost always wore a girdle. When we went to a coffee shop and then to the bathroom, she asked me for help getting it back up. She pulled up the front. I pulled up the back. We grunted and rocked back and forth, back and forth. Ooh! Ow! There! Just about got it, okay? Okay! We were grunting and sweating and laughing. Girdle on. We walked out of the bathroom, giggling like sisters with a secret.

Any conversation between Mommy and Daddy in these times always centered around child support. *Where is it? Why don't I see it? When will I see it? I don't have it now. When will you have it? These are your children. You can't just forget them when they're not around.* Child support. Child support. I got sick of hearing about it. But not as sick as not ever having the things that Child Support might have provided. Why didn't the law make my dad pay up? I never knew and I still don't.

We had a pretty, new blue Ford that Mom loved to drive. I don't know how she got it, but car payments were a struggle. She would park it a block or so away from the place where we got free food. She said if they saw her new car, they would think we had a lot of money and really didn't need the food. They gave us a big hunk of cheese, some peanut butter, cans of soup and crackers. These were called commodities, and we were always glad to get them.

Once Mom told Sissy to go buy some sauerkraut with money she had gotten for her birthday. Sissy said okay, then went for a walk to the Ben Franklin store instead of the grocery store. There she bought some trinkets and a rubber weenie. She forgot about the sauerkraut. Mommy was mad because we were hungry and needed the sauerkraut to go with the real weenies. So, we just had weenies. Mom told this story many times. Looking back at being poor, you had to laugh. Because we were resourceful, and we had each other. That was the most important thing, we all agreed. We sang the popular song back then, "*Oh, we ain't got a barrel of money. Maybe we're ragged and funny. But we'll travel along, singin' our song, side by side.*

Sissy was slow. Mom said she was just like all the other kids and should be treated the same. The school had special education to offer but Mom wouldn't allow it. "She's just like everyone else," she said. Mommy was stern. Her jaw became hard, and she looked cross when she said this. I knew there was something wrong, but I never said anything. I helped my sister. I tied her shoes. Later in life I taught her to drive, even though she was eight years older. Sissy cried often, holding me, and saying she loved me more than anything in this world. It made me feel sad and of course I said I love you too. I was always a little worried about her but never said anything to Mom about it. I would go out and play all the time and Sissy would stay indoors. She preferred to watch the soap operas and the westerns on TV.

Summers we went to visit Daddy in Oklahoma on the train. Sissy was always a little scared and never moved out of her seat. I liked to put my hands on the armrests and swing from seat to seat down the aisles to talk to passengers. Sissy would tell me don't talk to strangers. I said they weren't strangers. We are all going somewhere, and I like hearing where they're going and telling them about where I'm going, too. Sissy got angry when I did this. But she never got up from her seat. Sitting was her passion, I used to say, teasing unnecessarily. I would roam from car to car, having a good old time. It was always dark when we arrived in Oklahoma City. Once a storm was brewing and blowing everyone and everything around. I saw my daddy stride up the platform to meet us. My breath was taken, by the wind and by the sight of my daddy. His eyes were searching, his face so handsome, and my heart beat fast to see him. Daddy! Daddy! Over here! Our eyes met, he picked me up and swung me around. On the way home to his house, he talked to me about cars. He pointed out different styles, models, the "sequencia" taillights on the Thunderbirds. I learned to love cars and driving because that was what he loved. And I loved him.

Daddy was strong, with big muscles that burst through his shirt sleeves, that he liked to show off. He had coal black hair and lots of hair on his chest, too. His teeth were pearly white, and he was proud to say he'd never had a cavity. He played the harmonica, and he had lots of them, big and small. I watched my daddy as he would blow and draw the notes with flair and no music to look at. He raised his eyebrows, like smiling because his mouth was too busy. I loved visiting Daddy, except when he talked bad about Mommy. I never knew what to say, or how to act. Margie was my stepmom now. She told me don't ever upset Daddy. I knew this rule. But I didn't know how to not break it. Daddy got a bad headache sometimes. He sighed big and said, "I should have shot myself a long time ago." He would storm out of the trailer, slamming the door hard. I often felt his headache and his anger were my fault. I would shake in my body and wonder, *What did I do?*

When we went to visit, Mommy packed us just a few things. She said if we only have a couple of things, maybe he'll buy us some clothes, since he never sends child support. I told Daddy that I loved him all the time. He always said, "And I love *you*, Sugar." That made me happy. I thought to myself, *if only he would call me. If only he would come see me now and then.* But I tried not to think of these things, and I never said them. I didn't want to break the rule.

Daddy would get very upset with his stepson Ronnie. Ronnie was about Sissy's age, fifteen or so. He peed the bed occasionally, and Daddy would let him have it. He must have thought that yelling at Ronnie would teach him a lesson. But it didn't. I felt sorry for Ronnie. I said nothing. Sherry was my stepsister and I loved her. She was pretty, with soft brown hair and golden eyes and lips like a bow. She never yelled or cursed or said anything bad about Mommy. Margie was pretty and nice, with eyes that sparkled and a beautiful smile, but she said bad things about Mommy. I could never listen to anything bad about Mommy. I might explode and come at you. I did have a temper. It was rare but deadly. It has been a challenge to conquer my whole life.

Oklahoma Roots

Emery Green and Geraldine Simmons both sprung up from dry, red, Oklahoma dirt. That's what they said. Mom's family were "blue bloods," royalty from Jesus, the King of Kings. That's what my Papa said. She was the youngest of eleven children. Johnnie May came after her but died soon after birth. So, Mom was the baby. They lived like Indians, she said, just squatters in a two- room house with dirt floors. Mommy and Daddy got married when they were nineteen and eighteen. Daddy's daddy was a drunk and a diabetic and left when Daddy was very young. His mom was sixteen when he was born, the first of four boys. My dad was proud that he never ever touched alcohol. He said he knew better, and that if he got started, he probably wouldn't stop. Ma-Maw raised all four of her boys working in a restaurant and cleaning motel rooms. Her house was tiny but very clean. She was stern and independent and didn't smile much. When she did smile her eyes would twinkle and I'd think, *Ma-Maw should smile more.* But she was good and hardworking and never accepted anything from anybody, not even her own children. If Daddy and Margie took her out for lunch, Ma-Maw insisting on paying for her own meal. She never wanted to owe anyone anything. It was hard to give to her, she just wouldn't accept anything. Ma-Maw lived a couple of blocks from Mommy's mom and dad, my Granny and Papa.

When I stayed overnight with Ma-Maw I slept in the little bed on the back porch. She was always fully dressed when I woke up. Her dark, wavy hair with silver streaks was neatly combed and held with a soft hairnet. She would be cooking, and the smells moved over me like the Spirit: Bacon *and* sausage. Fried eggs. Biscuits and gravy. Coffee, tea and orange juice. It seemed Ma-maw had been up for hours. (She always had cookies and coffee when she first woke up.) Daddy and Margie would be here soon from wherever they have been staying. Daddy would say, "Man, it smells good in here." I put on my pink, flowery housecoat and climbed up to the table. "Let's eat, y'all," said Daddy. I ate till I was stuffed then went to change my clothes for the day. It was nice at Ma-maw's house, but I was always glad to say good-bye. Ma-Maw frowned and looked away when she kissed me goodbye. Maybe she was just sad, but I don't think so. I think I reminded her of my mom.

Just a couple of blocks from Ma-Maw's house, was Granny and Papa's house. Their little house had a dirt yard in front and a big garden in back, and an old outhouse they didn't use much since they got indoor plumbing. Granny liked to tell a story about Uncle Fred. When he was a kid, he used the outhouse, and a chicken pecked him on the behind. Uncle Fred stood up and burst through the door yelling, "Snakes! Snakes!" I stayed with them a couple of weeks in summer.

Granny had a big feather bed on the screened-in porch. The cousins liked to sleep there when it was warm. Granny lay in bed with us and told us stories. Granny slathered Ben-Gay on herself because she had arthritis. She would often say, "Ol' Arthur's been bothering me all day long." We'd say, "Arthur who, Granny?" "Arthur Ritis. Laughter. Now, settle down, Granny's gonna tell you a story.

Long, long time ago, afore your granny and papa were married, afore Oklahoma was even a state, just pure dee old red dirt territory. One night a storm come up. Ooh, it was a terrible storm! The wind was a whippin', the screen door was a slammin' back n forth, back n forth. The air was that kind of funny color of yella, you know the kind it gets right afore a storm. Your granny stepped out on the front porch and yelled at the wind, "Whooo's gonna sleep with me this dark and stormy night? And a voice down the road, across the holler and up the hill shouted so you could barely hear over the wind, "I will!"

Now, granny went back inside and begun to churn butter. I churned and I churned, and I churned. The wind was a'howlin', the screen door was a'slammin back n forth, back and forth, the rain was a blowin' sideways, the thunder and lightnin' were louder and closer, louder and closer. Lordy, young'ns, your granny was scared!!

I stepped out onto the porch and once again hollered, "Who's gonna sleep with me this dark and stormy night?" And a voice down the hill on this side of the holler, yelled, "I will!" Oh! I went back inside and kept churnin' butter. What else could I do? I churned and I churned and I churned and my stomach was a churnin' too. The wind was a whistlin' loud and strong, the thunder was a clappin' and the lightnin' was a flashin' so's I could see the screen door fly off the hinges. One more time I went to the door and yelled at the top of m'lungs, "Who's gonna sleep with me this dark and stormy night?" And a voice down the hill, this side of the holler and right at the edge of the porch said real loud, "I WILL!!!!"

We all screamed and held onto our granny. "And you know who it was?" said my granny with twinkly eyes and a toothless grin. "It was your grandpa!!"

A peach tree stood on the side of granny's house. I ate the peaches, then stroked my whiskers from eating the peach. This amazed me until I understood that it was fuzz from that peach! (Later I heard people say young boys had peach fuzz when their facial hair began to grow.) The wooden front porch was warm and smooth on my bare feet. Granny let me sweep it, just as the sun spilled onto the steps in early morning. The screen door creaked softly and slammed easy. I loved being at Granny and Papa's house. They were gentle and funny and never angry. When the sun went down Granny would sit on the porch, take down her hair and let me comb her silver and black strands. I was very gentle, and understood this was a privilege.

She liked to tell a story about me dancing on the dinner table when I was little. Papa said get down you'll fall. I said, "Papa, you talk too much," right before I fell into Papa's arms. We went to church every Sunday morning and evening. When Granny gave me a dime for the offering tied into the corner of a hanky, I said very loudly when they passed the plate, "No, Granny. I want to take it where I can get something *fer* it." Granny smiled then put the dime in. We walked to town where she bought me pretty, white sandals. We walked to the pool and ate Frito Pies beside the pool. You could never say a bad word at Granny's, not even gosh or darn. Folks used to say that Granny and Papa were the best Christians they ever knew.

On the Skids

Mom worked as a waitress at a place called "La Duc's" and the Colonial Dinner House. It was there she met Lou. Lou Skidmore had a smooth face and thin reddish-brown hair. He wore suits and had a low, creepy laugh. Lou never said much to me; he was glued on my mom, who tolerated his attentions. She never said she loved him, although he would beg her to. After a few drinks Lou's eyes became red and filled with tears of devotion. He got down on one knee and looked up at Mommy, reminding me of a puppy. Mommy turned the other way, and I could tell she didn't love him, nor would she ever.

I put up with Lou because he bought me stuff. This is the default setting for any child who knows poverty. When you see opportunities to get something you go for it. At least that was the case with me and any other child I ever knew. Here was the game plan: At the restaurant's gift shop, I'd see something I wanted. I would beg Mommy for it, till Lou can't stand anymore begging. He would end up buying me what I wanted, and I would stay quiet for a while. Finally, Mommy couldn't stand all this begging (from Lou and from me) and agreed to get married. We lived in Kickapoo, Missouri, outside of Springfield, in a small house. I went to kindergarten for a time. Then, somewhere, somehow, Mom met another man whose name was also Lou, or Lewis. Lewis Browning. But everyone just called him Sag. He got the name from a football accident where he lost his front tooth. After that, everyone called him Snaggletooth, then Snag. Then when he got a new tooth, the name turned into Sag.

I liked Sag. And I liked to sneak around and say (when Lou was around) in a sing-song-y way: S-a-g spells Sag. I didn't like Lou. I knew my mom didn't love him and he never really paid me much attention. The main thing was, he was not my daddy. Daddy Sag wasn't either, but Daddy Sag wasn't Lou, and that made him okay in my book. Sag invited Sissy and me to call him that. He showed us his house in the little town of Verona. He had a daughter my age named Janice, but I never met her. Daddy Sag never saw her either, that I knew of, and he never talked about her. His marriage to Mom was his third, which should probably have been a red flag. Pretty sure, too, like my own father, he never paid child support. Dads need to pay child support. Out of sight, out of mind should never apply to children.

Sag liked going to the tavern downtown and taking my mom there. It is in this place my mom began to drink. She learned to like beer and she loved to dance. Daddy Sag said she was a natural born flirt, which caused them trouble. Something was exciting about Daddy Sag and Mom to me. Maybe it was because Mom was already married. Later she never talked about her marriage to Lou. It was short and didn't account for much, Mom said. I was glad to leave the world of Lou for the world of Lewis. And, I liked saying, "Daddy Sag." Daddy Sag was kind to my sister. He put up with the younger daughter, and I put up with him, too. He wasn't Daddy, but he was a step up from the other guy. We moved to the little garage house in time for school to start. It was a new direction for the ragtag threesome of Mommy, Sissy, and me, the "displaced persons" that Mom would sometimes call us. I of course didn't understand what that referred to. I doubt if she did either.

Daddy Sag's mother lived in the big house on the other side of the garden. It was a nice white house with a porch swing, a dining room, and a kitchen with an electric stove. It was cheery and much nicer than the garage house we live in. Her name was Verla, and she was very cranky. She had rheumatoid arthritis, and was severely crippled by it, although she could get around with effort. She walked bent over crooked and her legs were stiff as she shuffled. She had knuckles big as doorknobs. Mom said she'd be cranky too if she had these problems. She always tried to be nice to Verla, but Verla was cold and grumpy most of the time. She invited Mommy to play canasta with her and her friends. Everyone smoked when they gathered around the table. I sometime sat in and watched the smoking and playing. I learned here how to shuffle and deal cards. Mama smoked very daintily, like she knew she wasn't supposed to be smoking. She barely drew in the smoke then blew it out slow, like a secret.

On the Skids

Sissy, Daddy Sag and Me in the little Garage House

Once when I was older, Grandma Verla bent over to pinch off some dead flowers. I did it, too. The cigarettes I had lifted from someone's package in the card game fell from my bra onto the ground. Grandma Verla was stern and told me to get my own cigs. It wasn't long before I did just that. One time I stood by a fountain with beautiful colored lights in downtown Springfield. There was a soft wind that blew my hair as I stood by the fountain, and it made me feel beautiful, too. I told Grandma Verla this little story and she laughed, saying nothing. I never spoke to her again about such things. I never talked to her much at all, really. I thought Grandma probably missed her real granddaughter, Janice.

Surprising Meanness

In first grade in Verona, we sat in little chairs in a circle and learned to count and clap and sing songs. When it rained, we played indoors. Once I tossed a big soft ball up to the ceiling and broke a light. I panicked and told my teacher, Mrs. Rider through my tears, that my mommy couldn't afford to pay for it. She wanted me to stop crying so she slapped me. It hurt but I stopped crying. One day, not long after that, Mrs. Rider was about to go into the restroom just as I was coming out. I opened the door fast and knocked her glasses off. I said I was sorry, but I really wasn't. I just knew Mrs. Rider was not a warm person who cared about children, at least not me. These things stay with you. Why did I cry in front of her? I had no reason not to, and crying was the normal response in fear of causing my mother distress. I worried about my mother. I'm not sure if she worried about me. She counted on me, I knew that much. She turned to me, she leaned on me, and she "loved me with all her heart."

When I left for school Mommy would call out, "Make a hundred!" And I usually did. In second grade, on a test, there was a fill-in-the-blank part. One question said, "I wish I had _____." I put "a boyfriend." Mrs. Wilson frowned and said that wasn't nice. I wasn't supposed to be thinking about boys at my age. This seemed like the beginning of innocently saying the wrong thing at the wrong time. I'd like to say I learned my lesson about that. But it's not true.

Occasionally, Mom would leave me with friends and neighbors, people she worked with. A bunch of us stayed at the home of Judy Brown, who was a kind of magnet for kids, a professional babysitter, of sorts. Now you would say she owned her own childcare business. Judy's mother Betty lived with her, and she was blind. She got around just fine there in her familiar surroundings; she felt her way around the house with her hands and her quiet sense of direction without much trouble. She slid her feet in and out of the slippers by her bed, never fumbling. All the kids worked their way around Judy's mother. It was chaotic there at times, but like all kids, I made my way too, trying to stay out of the way and still have a good time.

Judy's friend was named Nola. Big Nola, they called her. Big Nola sat in an overstuffed chair with the stuffing coming out on the sides, mainly due to the cats who came in and out, scratching every scratchable surface.

Surprising Meanness

I thought, too, maybe because of Big Nola never moving out of that chair, except to answer the door occasionally. Nola was big and soft, and both kids and cats like to jump up on her and lodge themselves for a little rest. I was no different.

One day I was snug as a bug in a rug up there on Big Nola's lap, and I was telling her secrets. I didn't think it was such a bad thing that I told her. I was feeling cozy and safe and happy to be near a grownup with her attention. I whispered in her ear that sometimes I peed in the bathtub. Big Nola opened her eyes wide and her mouth even wider. Then I guess because she didn't know how else to make clear how unacceptable that kind of thing was, she slapped my face. Hard. Of course I now know (and knew then, to a degree) that peeing in the bathtub is *not okay*, but it seems to me that revealing something like that isn't anything that merits a physical reaction, especially when the words roll out from a sense of intimacy and fun. I thought my secret was safe with Big Nola. I thought there was something kind of funny about my story. I was wrong.

For many years I lived with the sensation that someone would slap me if I got too cozy with them, if I told them anything "unacceptable." From this experience I learned that trauma is real. Even if you try to minimize or deny it, it creeps up in odd ways, like a strange replay of sensation, like a ghost.

Daddies, Various

On Saturdays Daddy Sag would go get a haircut and then to the beer joint in Monett. He would take me with him sometimes. We got into the fat old Chrysler and revved up the engine. Daddy Sag drove with a can of beer between his legs. He poured the beer into his mouth like a pitcher. I could see the sun shining through the yellow, making it golden. *How does he do that?* I wondered. Daddy Sag would point out things on the road to me, and say things like, how many of them people are dead in the cemetery? I don't know. All of 'em. He sang me a song called "Mares eat Oats."

> Oh, mares eat oats and does eat oats
> And little lambs eat ivy
> A kid'll eat ivy, too
> Wouldn't you?

I liked going with him. He might drop me off at the pool if I thought to bring my suit, which I always did. All alone, I swam and jumped up and down and did somersaults till I was exhausted and red as a lobster. Mom would pick me up later. Most of the time, though, I waited for him to get his hair cut, (which he did every week, no matter what, even though his hair was quite short), then go to the tavern around the corner (maybe that was the real reason). In the tavern it was cool and dark. It had signs behind the bar that said, "Drink like Helen B. Happy," and "We Reserve the Right to Refuse Service to Anyone", and "Everyone Deserves Another Shot." I was proud of my reading at age six. I could barely read the songs on the jukebox, but I could always read the letters and numbers. I didn't know what song I would hear but I liked almost all of them. My favorites were G11, "Stranger on the Shore" and B14, "Music, Music, Music."

Mr. McDonald was my music teacher in school and like a daddy to me. In fourth grade I picked out my instrument, a clarinet. I liked playing and marching in the band. When the sheet music to Zenith flew off my music clamp, Mr. McDonald ran to get it. "That's okay, it's okay," I said. "I don't need it." Turned out I wasn't reading the music. I was playing the song by ear. Was this a good thing or a bad thing? I didn't know. And I never had the chance to find out. Mom tried to get my real daddy to

Daddies, Various

make the payments for my clarinet, but he didn't. They came a few times to the house for the payment. Mom and I hid behind the couch. "Shhh," Mommy whispered. "Don't say a word." I was good and said nothing. Bam, bam, bam!!! "Mrs. Browning! We know you're in there," said the man loudly. We were silent. Then they left. But they got my clarinet anyway. They came and got it at my school.

We watched a lot of television while Mom was working, especially in summer. There was Make Room for Daddy, Father Knows Best, and Opie and Andy. I could whistle the theme song from the Andy Griffith show. From Daddy Danny I learned dads could be funny and makes mistakes. From Daddy Robert I learned Father knows the answers to most questions, especially ones that come up in families. I thought I'd like to ask my daddy questions. Like, "Why did you leave? Why don't you call me?" Mom kept asking him on the phone now and then, "Where's the child support?" It never came. Daddy Andy taught me that life can be funny, it's best to be gentle, and forgiveness is always the way to go. Barney was silly, funny, faithful and respectful of Daddy Andy's wise advice. Opie was like me, always curious, always wondering why. We watched sometimes till 2 o'clock. We had to get up then and clean the house, because our mom got home from work by three.

My favorite TV Daddy was Jack LaLanne. He was my physical consultant, my health instructor, and my TV daddy. I put on my red stretchy swimsuit to work out with him and his dog named Happy. Working out with Jack made me happy, too. It made me love exercise. It made me believe in good people, even daddies. Jack called us students and I liked that. I felt he was talking straight to me. He told me I could stay healthy and live a long life. He said that being happy isn't about being rich. It's about being healthy and once he told me a story about people in Central America who sang on the bus. They weren't rich, but they were happy. That's how I wanted to be. I have always thanked God for physical exercise and being outside with the trees and birds. Inside with Jack, I got a good workout. Outside, I felt at home and happy to be alive and alone.

We played card games like Slap Jack and Old Maid. Sissy would lie on the floor, pick me up with her feet on my chest and fly me around holding my hands. Sometimes she let go of my hands and I would fly to the floor. This is what we did to avoid being too bored.

Once, on a lovely summer's day, my sister went a little crazy. She took the garden hose, turned it on full blast, and sprayed the living room through the screen door. Was she trying to clean the floor? Did she just think it was funny? I laughed at first but then it wasn't funny. She finally stopped and Mom came home to find the place a big mess. Daddy drove from Oklahoma to Missouri, and they put my sister in the hospital. She had a lot of tests and got some medication. Daddy blamed Mommy, saying Sissy should never be left home alone, especially with me. Mommy said if he would help with child support maybe she wouldn't have to leave us alone to go to work all the time. It never really got settled, but that never happened again. They did argue about it several times, when they had to speak on the phone a few times a year. That, and of course child support.

A Daughter's Reflection

She loved him with the absent, fantasy-filled love of a lonely child. Closing her eyes, she saw him coming toward her in the sunshine – arms open, smiling always, perfect teeth flashing a joy in seeing her and her alone. He would scoop her up, yes, scoop her right up and cradle her in his giant muscular arms. There she would nestle down in perfect peace and comfort, wishing only to never leave, never to be far apart again. For being far apart would mean him forgetting her.

He forgot her often [or so it seemed]. She would dream of receiving gifts, phone calls, birthday cards and letters in the mail, surprise visits to the zoo or an amusement park. These things never happened, of course, only in her perfect dreaming of something she might have seen in a movie. But when she saw him, she knew she was loved, she just knew it, although looking back, there was so little evidence. But that never stopped her from believing.

She did not want to be forgotten and so she struggled many times to make sure no one did forget her. She was compelled to answer every question in school. She sometimes played dumb to hold the teacher's attention. She spoke up at odd times, like when conversations had nothing to do with her and she would interrupt. This was tiring, burdensome and not at all fun (though she often seemed to be having fun). She would always come back to the perfect love that she imagined through the prism of her hazy memories and imagined scenarios.

She remembered at least three things: His handsome face, his clever jokes that made her laugh and his bitter stories that made her cry. He talked about her cruel and deceitful mother, how unfair life was to him, how he had always tried so hard, but life never seemed to give him a break. He would relay incidents in which he always won the argument, which included telling his opponent, "Wait just a cotton-pickin' minute here." Or, "I said, 'Look, this is the way it is, friend, and I don't mean maybe'." He very often punctuated his sentences with "I don't mean maybe." This underscored his seriousness, his superiority, and masculinity. Sometimes he gritted his perfect teeth while saying it. He would talk about these things, and she would cry. She would cry and not really know why she cried. She felt as though she was being crushed somehow. Sobs came and he looked at her quizzically. He would sigh, look away and say, "I should have shot myself a long time ago." This only increased the crying. Later she thought she cried because she didn't know what to do when he spoke like this. She thought she cried because she knew she was supposed to listen but there were so many things she wanted to say. She wanted to say things, too, but she never got to. Only little words here and there, through tears and sobs.

Once in the auto body repair shop where he worked alone all day, he tried to convince her that there was no such thing as the present moment. Look, he said, pointing to his watch. The moment has gone by just as you're looking. And all we can do is remember it. There's no present, only the future and the past. This made her think hard through the years. Then she eventually challenged it by concluding for herself that there was no such thing as the future and no past either, only the present moment. Poor him, she thought. (Another thing about him: intelligent, but not too smart. That's how he liked it. No one could challenge him. He saw to that by keeping distance, being clever and intimidating.)

He kept getting married and divorced. Four times he said I do. And then…he didn't. But he had to keep getting married. Otherwise, who would cook for him? Who would laugh at his stories, listen to his rants, wash and iron his work clothes? Who would smile with adoring eyes and perfect love, never crossing him, never speaking up, never saying, No. YOU wait just a cotton-pickin' minute! I have something to say, and I don't mean maybe. I have something to say and I'm going to say it and you're going to STOP TALKING and LISTEN. JUST LISTEN. Sometimes she imagined that she would tie him up. Tie him up, like in the westerns. Put a sock in it then tie a bandana over his mouth and around his head. Tell him a thing or two.

Like what about all those birthdays you missed? And how the hell could it always be Mom's fault, the other guy's fault, the government's fault? What makes you so perfect and wonderful and innocent all the dang time? And guess what? I've been doing some pretty impressive things in my little life. How'd you like to hear about 'em? Well, just let me tell you a cotton-pickin' thing or two, yes sir-ee bob. And I don't mean maybe.

Ah, but she loved him. His gentle laugh, his twinkly eyes, his endless play on words. His smile when she said something a little clever or silly. Occasionally get in a word edgewise. I could have told you that, if I had just known it, she said once. She said that and he chuckled. He thought that was a little funny. How she longed to show him that she could be funny, too. She was a lot like him, if only he could know that. If only he could shut up long enough to notice her, really see her. Her heart ached for this.

Another time she heard him talking about her to someone. Why that is one of the most resourceful little gals you'd ever want to meet, he said. SHE was resourceful. He knew that about me, she thought. He knew I was

A Daughter's Reflection

RESOURCEFUL!! *This filled her with glee. Maybe he DOES know me. Maybe I seeped into his awareness, and I didn't even notice it myself!* She loved him so, much more than she had thought.

Once, she brought home to meet him the man she thought she would marry. Both she and her future husband tried to engage the elder in meaningful conversation. It was challenging, she knew it would be, for she had chosen a quiet man. She had chosen someone who didn't hold forth, didn't dominate the interactions, didn't necessarily know everything… She had chosen someone who could look at her and say, *Ah! Very interesting…I didn't know that*. She had searched far and wide to find someone like that. And when she found him, she talked and talked and talked and talked. And, sometimes, she was a little frustrated that he didn't say much. But not too frustrated. Because, now here they were, in front of HIM. HE who talked without ever taking a breath. HE, who got up and left the room, if the conversation didn't interest him, or have to do with him. HE, who started playing his harmonica and then stopped when my friend picked up his guitar to jam along.

I wish you lived close by, said the dad to his daughter years later. *I wish you could come around, go out to eat with us, bring the kids over sometime. Oklahoma is nice,* he said. *Come live in the flat, open space of family restaurants, pick-up trucks, country music and old-time religion. Oh yes, that would be great,* she said, humoring him. *That would be perfect.* That'll be the day, she thought.

Hillbilly Diet

I liked hanging out in the back booth while Mom worked. The booths were red and bouncy, sometimes with crumbs in the crease of the seat and the back. I could read a book or just look around at people, read the menu or play the jukebox that hung on the wall over the table. Sissy and I would stop by an hour or so before she got off. On every menu of course were hamburgers. That was a favorite but couldn't come close to the "Hot Beef Sandwich," which Mom said was healthy. "Eat this for strength," she would say. So, naturally I always ate beef to feel better and stronger. What a creation: two slices of white bread, one flat in the middle of the plate, the other cut into triangles, nestled on the sides. On top were hot slabs of roast beef, and on top of that sat a perfect scoop of mashed potatoes. The crowning glory was loads of smooth and delicious hot brown gravy. I have always admired vegetarians and tried to be one for a few months when I was older. It didn't work out, as I was always thinking, "I need beef to feel better." And it has always been the case that I feel better, clearer and stronger after eating a nice slice of beef!

Having only one car, we often took Daddy Sag to work on Saturday mornings. I liked sneaking into the back and crouching down on the floorboard so that I could pop up when Daddy Sag got out of the car. "Surprise!" I squealed to my not-so-surprised mom. I tumbled over the front seat, and we went straight to the Daylight Donut Shop. The puffy, sugary, still warm from the oven glazed donuts were thrilling to my taste buds. One, two, three, four, however many I wanted. That one day, Mom and I ate half a dozen each. It wasn't hard. "It's mostly air," Mom said. That sounded right.

Candy was my friend. Downtown Verona there was BB Hamm's store. BB Hamm was a slight old man, bent over from the kind of arthritis Daddy Sag's mom, Verla had. But BB got around quickly. He shuffled all over his Dry Goods store, where there was just about anything you could think of available for purchase, including, of course, candy. There was a giant candy case as you walked in the door on your left, whose bell rang, announcing your arrival in the store. As far as I know, no one worked in BB Hamm's but BB himself. So that bell was essential. Walking on the creaky wooden boards would give your presence away, if he didn't hear the bell. I walked downtown to get milk, bread, coffee for Mom, and candy for me, naturally. Butterfingers were my favorite.

Hillbilly Diet

Contenders were Pay Day, Snickers, Cherry Mash, and Sugar Daddys. Sugar Daddys were great because they could last for hours. Focusing on that long, caramel-laden sugar on a stick absorbed my attention and made me feel happy. I loved watching it disappear, slowly over time. It would change shape slightly, with a point at the end. I could circle that around my tongue if it got thin enough. Once in a while I bit a little part off the top. Mostly I just kept at it till it got down to the nub around the stick. Goodbye little stick. See ya next time! I turned to candy for solace, for comfort, and just for the thrill of sugar. When I was twelve, I went to the dentist for the first time. Every tooth in the back of my mouth had cavities. Every indulgence has its effects. There were no fluoride treatments at the time. Crest was there, but no flossing, and no one to nag me to floss, brush and rinse like I did with my kids years later.

At night instead of counting sheep, I sometimes counted the slices of bread I had eaten that day. I counted ten once and panicked a little. I noticed my belly getting bigger and bigger. This was not okay with me. But the carbs kept coming.

The Widening Circle

My best friends were two sisters and another girl. When I came to Verona, I was in first grade. When I was in second, Berta started school. Her sister Diana was in third. I was sandwiched in between with the girl in my grade, Carol Sue. Berta and Diana had a pretty, blue house down the road and across the cow pasture from me. The house was pretty outside, but inside was very messy. It seemed like Jane sat and smoked and read most of the time. But she was pretty and smart and had a gentle laugh. Later I wondered, *Was Jane depressed?* Berta and Diana had three other sisters, Bonnie, Becky, and Marsha. Bonnie lived in a home for special kids. We liked it when Bonnie came home, and we were all together. I pretty much adopted this family and they let me hang out with them, seems like all the blessed time. That's what I heard their dad Bob say one time, only he didn't say blessed.

For my eighth birthday, Mom got us a phone. She played a trick on me and told Berta and Diana to call me on it. She hid the phone and when it started ringing, I was shocked. I picked it up when I found it and Berta and Di said hello. Before that, if we wanted to call each other, we went out to the edge of the cow pasture and made Tarzan calls. The Tarzan calls were fun, and I missed them after the phone was installed.

Carol Sue had long, thick, straight auburn hair, like a horse's mane. Chubby and freckle-faced, she had smallish lips, not given to much smiling, except when it's okay to smile and laugh, like on the playground, in the house, or walking home together. Twinkly, blue eyes and a perfectly straight Irish nose, Carol Sue was serious, responsible, and very intelligent, with a totally silly and giddy streak that seems to come out mostly with me. Together we ran wild on the playground at Verona Elementary. It was a huge field, with three baseball diamonds and a running track, a basketball hoop, and a small, wooded hill beyond. We weren't supposed to go up there, but it was tolerated, as long as we came in from recess on time. We were happy out there on the playground, running, always running, in some way or another. We made up word games ("Let's say 'pppt' after every word, two times at the end of a sentence!"), we played hard on the merry-go-round and the jungle gym. We laughed so hard we could barely stand.

Once I fell off the top of the jungle gym and hit the back of my head hard on the ground. I jumped right up so no one would see that I fell. It was humiliating to fall, so I pretended I was fine. But I wasn't. For the rest of recess, I couldn't open my eyes. The light was so bright that my eyes stayed shut tight. I found my way to the side of the school building and just stood there, waiting. Why didn't I go to someone? Why didn't I ask for help? This pattern lay across much of my life in years to come. Being brave is good, being subversive about your own pain and difficulty is another. The irony is, sometimes it is good to say, "Nothing's wrong" even to yourself. But the pain can go undetected after a while and come out in surprising and harmful ways, like vision problems (which happened), like addiction (debatable), like a bad temper (yep), like feeling numb (oh yeah). Much later in life, I learned meditation. I learned stillness. And breathing with awareness. But then, it was just "keep going and keep smiling," which I did most of the time. Until I didn't. Truth, like stars, may be obscured, but always comes out, I found. With people, with everything.

After recess, Carol Sue went to work. It was harder for me to do that, and I admired her discipline. I was always wanting to go sharpen my pencil, get a drink of water, or go to the bathroom and look out the window. Carol was never concerned about being liked, it seemed. She focused more on her studies. I really wanted to be liked, and sometimes got the feeling I was but was never sure.

Berta and Diana's parents fought a lot. They drank and smoked all the time it seemed. They let us drink at their parties in the basement when we were older. The first time I drank at age fourteen, it was Seagram's 7 out of the bottle. I got smashed and very sick. I threw up on Berta's bed. Jane called the next day and told me I had to come and clean it up, which I did without protest. Natural consequences, I later learned. You might think I'd never drink again, with that experience. Not the case, as will become clear.

One night, Bob and Jane were fighting bad. Berta thought Bob was going to kill her mom. She ran to my house barefoot in the snow, across the cow pasture. I went back with Berta, and everyone was crying. Bob was gone for the night. After that, he didn't talk to me for a long time. I had to duck if we saw him on the road because Berta and Diana weren't supposed to run around with me anymore. Jane still liked me, and I could be at the house when Bob wasn't home. A long time after this, I was in the living room in the blue house. Bob walked in, smiled at me and said hello. I ran into the bedroom, crying, I was so happy.

Another time I thought Daddy Sag might kill my mom. There was so much fighting, screaming and knocking stuff over. I didn't know what to do, so I ran across the cow pasture to Jane and Bob's house. It was summer and I wasn't barefoot. They let me stay the night and things cooled off a bit the next day. Our fighting parents were a theme woven throughout our school years. Fighting and alcohol. It all seemed to go together.

It makes me laugh to see the calf walk down the path to take a bath. I first heard that funny little saying from my across-the-street neighbor who was my on-again off-again friend Dee in grade school. Dee's mother Barb was the one who said it. They moved to our town in fifth grade. I was so happy to have someone to play with move in across the street. We played tetherball endlessly and she always beat me, *always*. But I didn't care; it made *her* laugh to see me try so very hard to beat her. "I'm gettin' good, you better watch out," I'd say. "Oh, yeah?" she would answer with a sly grin. "Yeah," I would say, knowing she knows she'll beat me, no problem, me thinking the same thing, but hoping someday for a miracle. Dee was skinny, athletic, fast and worldly. I was soft and brainy, religious and awkward. She taught me how to shave my legs. Her stepdad Lee pierced my ears, first with clothespins, then with ice cubes after they closed up the first time. Dee wore eye make-up, thick lines of black goo from the corner of her eyelids, swooping outwards to a cat-like curl at the end. Sexy! She wore cinnamon-colored hose, held up by a very sexy garter belt, and white sneakers. Super-sexy!! She knew how to rat her hair so that it "poufed" perfectly on top. I thought she looked like Cleopatra. I knew I could never pull the look off. So, I didn't try. I just admired her from a distance and tagged along whenever I could.

On Saturday nights we would go to the Princess Theater in Aurora. The theater smelled like cigarette smoke, popcorn, old paint, and mold. We watched movies like Planet of the Apes, Psycho and the Blob. The movies weren't so important, I learned. It was just about getting together and of course, boys. The bathrooms were coated with graffiti. *Here I sit all broken-hearted, tried to --it but only -arted.* I was shocked by this. How could a *girl* have written it? Impossible. I love *Harold Deanie's Gold Bond weenie!! Mackie loves Janet. So says Janet. Laura B. is a whore!!* What is that? I didn't know but I knew it wasn't good. I had never seen or read or heard anyone say these kinds of things. My little church mouse mind was in a whirl. Once we were all sitting down in the front few rows and one of Maxie's friends from Aurora was mad. She said she knew someone didn't like her anymore and she didn't "give a goddamn!"

I had never heard anyone who wasn't a grown-up speak that way (and only a couple of grown-ups). I heard my mom say a bad word once in my life. So, when I heard this young lady say these words, I jumped up and said, "I'm not sittin' with a cusser!!" I moved to the back of the theater. Everyone looked at me in shocked amusement. It was lonely in the back of the theater and soon I moved back down with the girls.

Dee always laughed at me, and I kept coming back for more. I thought we were friends, but I was just the butt of her jokes and the clueless backdrop to her pretty wild life. I tagged along with her in grade school. She bullied me in high school. It didn't help me to be anywhere near her. Still, I was somehow attracted to what I thought was an exotic and dangerous kind of world she moved in.

Unhinged

Christmas was a scary time for Sissy and me. Scary because of the habits of my mom and stepdad. Where there was Christmastime there were nights out on the town. And where there were nights on the town, at taverns, mostly, there was drinking. And where there was drinking there was first dancing, then flirting, then dirty looks and harsh words. And where there were dirty looks and harsh words, not long after came the fighting. My mother and my stepdad fought, it seemed, all the blessed time. And around Christmas, the time of peace and goodwill on earth, it got worse, much worse. It seemed my mother, God bless her, could not stop her mouth from going and going. (Was this what Daddy meant?) Daddy Sag wasn't perfect, I knew that. But mom was always thinking he did something horrible. Maybe he did, but I never saw it, never having gone to the tavern with them together, just separately. It seemed Daddy Sag might have wanted to stop it and somehow didn't know how. Could he have enjoyed mom carrying on like that? I sometimes wondered in my little dark corner of fear and shaking. No, he did not like it, but he did not run from it. Or sometimes he tried, and Mom would block the doorway as if to say, "You will NOT be leaving until I say it is time to leave!"

Her name was Geraldine, but she was always Jere (like "Jerry") to everyone in Missouri. To folks in Oklahoma, she was Dean. To me, she was always Mom or Mama or Mommy. Sissy would call her mother when I was little, and she was in high school. Friends used to call each other "Kid" when Sissy was in high school. My sister sometimes got mixed up and called our mom Kid, then Mother, then "Kid Mother." We often laughed and used this name for Mom.

She was a very religious woman who somehow got caught up in all this boozing and fighting. The only time I heard her say a bad word was when she called Daddy Sag an "old fart" during a fight when he tried to get up and leave. She was good and kind, too. We would go out in the car sometimes to visit her friends. If no one was home, Mom wrote a note on one of her guest checks from the restaurant and stuck it in the door. They could see that it was from her from a distance, because the checks were green. "Just dropped by to say hello. Hope you're feeling better. See you soon!" *Just Jere*. When Mom cooked, she would often pack up a little food and send me out to deliver it to neighbors. I never wanted to and would complain. "Do I have to?" "Yes, you have to. It won't take you but a minute. Now, go on, and come right back." *Like I wouldn't have come right back.* It was usually cold when Mom did this, and I dreaded the cold. I would go, come back, warm up by the stove, and have my own meal. I never gave Mom any trouble until high school. Then I made up for any lost time.

When Mom and Daddy Sag would go out to the tavern, of course Sissy and I stayed home. Even though she was eight years older, Sissy was no more mature, due to whatever it was that happened to her at birth. The story never got straight, but when we were left alone at night, I would lay awake and worry and Sissy went straight to sleep. She thought I was silly to worry. She didn't feel like comforting or reassuring me. She loved me but she felt bad that she was eight years older than I was, and she was learning things from me. She would go up into the woods sometimes and sob and carry on. She would say out loud as she cried, "I wish, I wish, I wish…" I wondered what it was that Sissy wished. I wondered if it had anything to do with me. Sometimes I felt she wished I hadn't been born. She could be mean and hurtful by laughing at me or looking at me with mean eyes. We had a game we played sometimes that I later felt bad about. I would tell her that I was her midget mother. I told her that our mom was really our grandmother. It was a fantastic story that was amusing to Sissy but also probably confused her and made her sad. Sissy would sometimes cry and hold me so tight I couldn't breathe. And other times, she took pleasure in making me cry.

It was cold around Christmas, naturally. It was beautiful, too, outside our little converted garage house. When my parents would come in after their night of fun, they turned into the gravel driveway and I could hear the crunch of tires that told me they were home, even as they turned off their lights so as not to shine into the house and wake us up, as if I could ever sleep. I always stayed awake, heart pounding, imagining the worst. What if they had a wreck? What if he hurt or killed my mother? Because, when he had had enough, he would slam her. He would slam her, and she would punch him, and he would punch her back, and on and on. Then she would scream and summon someone (usually me) to call the cops and sometimes I would and here they would come, and we were all (my sister, mother and I) crying and it looked as if my mean old stepdad was the worst man in the world, and… Where was he? Probably he had escaped by then, out back to the mountain, or the ponds or the chicken house, or maybe some other hideaway I never knew about. Anyway, there would be broken glass, turned over furniture, a shattered window, sometimes some blood, but thankfully, nothing ever too serious, which was amazing.

When I heard them turn into the driveway my heart was calmed and re-excited in the span of a few seconds. It was calmed that they were finally home, and I could stop thinking they were dead from a fight or a car wreck. But re-excited about what they might do to each other now that they were home and out of public sight. I waited in the darkness of my little bed. Why aren't they coming in? It's cold out there. Later, I found out that alcohol warms you, or makes you numb enough to not know or care about how cold you are. What are they doing? I knew by now that they liked to just sit out there and fight in the comfort of the car. If they came inside, they might have to be quiet, but not really. If they had had enough booze, they would fight on into the night. My sister could sleep through anything. I could sleep through nothing, so even if they whisper-fought, I would only get up and listen through the curtains that separated the front room from where we all slept. I had to know what was going on. So, sometimes I got up and went out there, to the car. I would pound on the windows, and beg them to come in. Sometimes, Mom would open the car door and let me in, like on that one Christmas. She held me on her lap and tried to get me to stop shaking. I couldn't stop. Finally, they did come in. The Christmas tree was blinking so pretty in front of the dark frosty window. The bubble lights gurgled their colorful nativity: peace and goodwill, peace and goodwill... The shouting grew louder. My pleading grew with it. "Stop it, please, Daddy Sag! Please don't hurt mommy! I'll do anything. Please don't! Please!" And then it happened. Some kind of movement, a thud, a gasp and a hoarse scream. The tree, the beautiful tree, was toppled and glass, water, lights and pine needles were everywhere in the otherwise dark and chaotic room. "Call the cops, call the cops!" my mom gasped. I thought to myself and said to no one, *Nothing like this should ever happen.*

Chickens and Church

In winter we had the big potbelly stove. Sissy and I collected kindling all autumn long, just sticks fallen from the trees in the yard. Ed Start had a furniture factory across the street. It was a long, low building, a one-man operation, as far as I could see. Ed made end tables and coffee tables, blonde ones, with slightly tapered legs and not-so-solid tops, very pretty and modern, I thought. He gave us kindling, too, just scraps, plenty good enough for our little operation. You could see the fire by opening the door or through the grate that was the facing of the door. So comforting, so warm, was the heat that came from that little stove. If you stood close, you'd make your skin too hot on one side and too frosty on the other. So, you had to just keep turning. One winter Daddy Sag brought home a box full of baby chicks, just about the most exciting thing a kid could hope for, except for maybe a puppy. The chicks chirped loudly and seemed to enjoy being held. My heart was happy holding them.

When we went outside of course we bundled up. Whenever we didn't have gloves, we had socks on our hands. I thought my mom was very clever to think of socks on our hands to keep them warm. The thought of hands and feet in reverse made me smile.

Every night I had to say the following to my mom: "Good night, sweet dreams, I love you, you're the sweetest mommy in the whole world." She didn't make me say it. I made it up and if I didn't say it, I got scared. I thought something bad might happen, to her, to me, or to both of us. If I forgot and went to bed, I had to get up and say it or she had to come in and let me say it. It was a ritual that lasted a long time.

In summer the chicks were all grown up. Our rooster was called Dancer. Daddy Sag showed us that if you tickled him under his wings he would dance. Under Dancer's wings it was warm and alive. He strutted around the chicken coop with pride. I thought for sure there was no other rooster like him.

For my birthday I got a pair of Banty (Bantam, I later learned) chicks. I named them Romeo and Juliet. It was fun having chickens and gathering eggs.

At night Mom would send me outside to toss the slop. It was beautiful at night, with the stars popping out as the sun went down and the smoke from the trash barrel swirling up to the sky. I loved being alone there in the back of the house. If it was cold, I could see my breath next to the fire and pretend to smoke. If it was warm, lightning bugs held my attention and made me think about God. I thought, *God is good. The world is full of beauty. I am happy here, with God, with the beauty.* And *I am surrounded by God's beauty. I am filled with God's love.* These weren't affirmations. They were natural thoughts that made me feel life's sweet embrace. These moments were the groundwork of a lifelong love of solitude. Being alone gave me peace, joy, and clarity. They connected me to a faith I could call my own. But of course I didn't know that until years later.

Mom and Daddy Sag sent us to Sunday School at the First Christian Church. For a while we had a preacher named Rusty Winterfield. He was young and tall with short blonde hair. His smile made me happy and a little woozy. Rusty was on fire for the Lord. After Sunday school, at the end of worship, he came down from the pulpit with his Bible. He waited for someone to join him and want to be saved. I felt bad for Rusty because I don't remember anyone going down for the altar call. I sat there thinking about what would happen if I got up and just started dancing. But I never wished to get saved. Not yet.

After church we came home, and Daddy Sag made us dinner. Daddy Sag was a good cook. He made good fried chicken and great pinto beans with fried taters and cornbread, which my mom also made. Daddy Sag taught us a trick that made the beans taste divine: a tablespoon of sugar! This Sunday the meal was chicken. Sissy and I sat down and dug in. After a few delicious bites, my sister said, "Well, you don't have to ever worry about Dancer again. "Why?" I asked. Her eyes twinkled as she said, "'Cause you're eatin' him." I stood up from the table, ran to Mom's bed, threw myself down and cried my eyes out. This was the way Sissy liked to be mean. She must have hurt so bad inside at times that being mean was the way she could feel better. She liked to spill secrets that weren't hers to spill. She liked to shock in ways that hurt and got others off balance. Like running to the bed, throwing yourself down, and crying till you're wrung out.

Mom made sure that we went to church every week. Granny and Papa were long-time members of the Church of Christ, the "one true church." Mom believed this and would have sent us to the Church of Christ, had there been one in the town of Verona. They decided that the closest thing to it was the First Christian Church, also known as the Disciples of Christ. The church was within walking distance, down the hill from our house to the right on the corner. It was small and white with a steeple and a few stairs leading up into the sanctuary. The sanctuary smelled like wood and communion. The pulpit was down front center, with the choir loft right beside it. The piano player Donna Gay was pretty and petite. I never heard her talk, just smile and play the piano. Once, she forgot about the Daylight Savings time change and was almost late. That was the only time I saw Donna Gay ruffled. She made it just barely. I was relieved for her and thought it made church interesting that day. Church was the center of life for so many folks back then. There were suppers and games and songs and laughter. My recollection of my church was, however, not deeply religious. Rusty tried hard with folks because that's just who he was as a messenger of God. It was much later in my own life as a minister that I understood what must have been his frustration with those whose faith is mostly a social lifestyle, with little emphasis on spiritual growth, which can be challenging, exciting and joyful.

Across the street from our church was the more beautiful and sort of scary-looking Catholic church. Catholics and Protestants didn't mingle much. Daddy Sag called them "cat-lickers," which I thought was an ugly word. When he said it, I looked down and pretended not to hear him. The carelessness of his words reflected the times and the effect of harsh words on the way folks get along, both locally and on a grander scale. Prejudice seems innocent until and unless you realize the humanity of "the other." But to Daddy Sag, and others around us, it was natural and harmless. The Catholic church was dark, inviting and mysterious. It was open all the time during the day for prayer. Once Carol Sue and I sneaked inside for just a couple of minutes. There were red candles flickering in the dark, exotic smells from incense, and amazing stained-glass windows. Mother Mary stood with her arms open wide and I thought she was beautiful. When I heard about confession on Thursday afternoons, I wished that I had confession. I often felt I had done something bad and didn't quite know what it was. I thought having someone to hear my confession would be a good thing, help me to be forgiven for whatever it was I might have done that lay hidden deep in my heart and I had somehow forgotten.

One Sunday, Mom and I drove down to Fayetteville, Arkansas to hear the famous evangelist, Jimmy Allen. He was preaching the beginning of a revival. Night after night there was preaching at revivals. Preaching and singing and at the end, the invitation to go down to the altar. The invitation was to confess your sins and devote your life to living for Jesus. To proclaim Jesus as your Lord and Savior. Brother Jimmy preached good, loud then soft. Pointing his finger and clutching his Bible. I was a little scared but loved what he was saying, loved it so much I didn't think about anything else at all. Mom hadn't been to church for a long time. She said she was afraid to go. Especially, she didn't want to take communion because she was too sinful. Maybe Mom could have used a priest to confess to, too. But she loved the evangelist Jimmy Allen, who I had never heard of but of course went along. I would go anywhere with Mom. When we were driving together, we were almost always happy. So down south we went, to hear "Brother Jimmy." I felt happy to be walking into church with my mom. It was the first time, and my heart was bursting with pride. We were sitting down close to the front and Brother Jimmy had preached his heart out. He got the job done with me. The Spirit tugged on me and told me to get down there. Maybe, just maybe, I could confess whatever I needed to and feel much better. This was exciting. I said to Mom, "I gotta go." She just looked straight ahead, nudged me a little and said, "Just go." And I did.

Mom had been searching for a Kleenex and for some reason I thought I needed to say, "Mom, you can't smoke in here." She looked cross and whispered to me fiercely, "I know that!" After going down front, and all the tears and singing and praying, I did feel wonderful. I was escorted to the back of the front of the church and told to put on a white robe. I was nervous but happy. My mom was with me, and she could see now that I would go to heaven. I stepped down into the cool water and was greeted with the warm smile of Brother Jimmy. He asked me if I repented of my sins and accepted Jesus as my Lord and Savior. I looked up with great seriousness and said, "Yes, I do." Down I went with Brother Jimmy's hand over my face with a white cloth. He told me to close my eyes and hold my breath. I thought about telling him that I was a good swimmer and could go underwater without my nose being held, but I didn't say it. Everything went quickly. When I came up out of the water, I felt like a newborn baby. People kindly helped me out of the pool and gave me my clothes. When I saw Mom, she was smiling through tears. "Why are you crying, Mommy?" She said she wasn't crying, she just had smoke in her eyes. She said that a lot. On the jukebox at the tavern, I found that song ("Smoke Gets in Your Eyes") and played it in future days. We ate at the AQ Chicken House in Springdale, Arkansas on the way back to Missouri. It was a happy time for me. On the way home, we sang hymns.

I really thought of myself as a Christian after that day. There were a lot of differences between what was said in church and how people acted

Chickens and Church

at home and school. I noticed these differences and thought about them a lot. The thing that stuck with me the most that I heard again and again was, "God is love." Well, if God is love, I thought to myself, then everyone believes. Because everyone believes in love, at least some kind of love. They also said, God is everywhere. God lives in everyone. I loved this theme and wanted to talk about it with all my friends, and later on, my dates. Sometimes it was a problem, but many times, it was a good conversation starter. On top of the nut mill downtown it said, "The eyes of the Lord are in every place, beholding the evil and the good." Later I learned that's in Proverbs, Chapter 15, verse three. When walking downtown I always walked by the nut mill and definitely felt that I was being watched. I wondered which category God placed me in. There were always shifting moments, when I felt good and walking in sunshine, and times when I felt evil and walking in cold shadows. I was very curious how I could keep the sun shining. But there were always dark invitations, it seemed. And sometimes, I just felt dark no matter what I had or hadn't done.

Rusty preached a great sermon one Sunday. He put a chair up front and had someone tie string around him. The sermon was about sin. He said it was like a string that someone ties around you. At first, you can break free from it, no problem. But if the string goes around again and again, it becomes very hard to break free from. Then you start walking around with a chair on your back. And you wonder why you feel so heavy, so burdened. I took this sermon very seriously. It stayed with me my whole life. I wanted to walk straight, with no chair on my back. I tried to say no to all the strings that might keep me from breaking free. But so many times, I forgot. That's when I needed that confession booth. Baptism was great, but confession, I found, was still necessary. Of all the choices there were about what to become in life, I wanted to be good. This was a driving force that I probably took too far. Wanting to be good can lead to pretending to be good. This isn't good. And it can stick to you in uncomfortable and sad ways. Dividing life into good and bad, right and wrong, even saved and unsaved can split your perception. It can divide people into camps. And it can create a false sense of self that cannot take criticism or deal with conflict. Churches, I have learned, are very susceptible to this split of perception that can lead to harsh judgement of self and others. It can also feel burdensome and secretive, having to "look good," even if you're not all that good. A conundrum of the faithful, no matter how good you are.

Dreams, Various

The girl had dreams at night that woke her up and she could only describe them to her mother as "millions." "I dreamed about millions again last night, Mommy," she would say with some anxiety, hoping to be understood, or at least acknowledged for not being crazy. There was a thread she hoped to get hold of by sharing it, a thread that provided a way back to now, to this room, to furniture and cereal and clothing and the warmth of her mother's arms and smile.

"Millions of what, honey?" replied mom. Inside herself she sighed. Not this again, she thought. Not because she didn't want to be helpful, but because she hadn't a clue how to be. It was so much easier dealing with real stuff, stuff like hunger, scraped knees and spelling words. But millions? That was out of her depth.

"Millions of everything: faces, trees, birds, words..." "Hmmm," her mother said. "Are you okay now?" "Yes, I think so." "Good. Time to get ready for school."

The girl wished her mother more curious. More often than not, in these conversations she would walk away and think, "I shouldn't have said anything at all. I should just keep everything to myself." And in the years to follow she often did. It was like a whole world in there, inside her head. It was soft and quiet and interesting and sometimes funny. But it could be frightening, wondering if she was all right. Wondering if others had dreams of millions, fantasies of weird and funny scenarios like stripping and dancing in church or being up there on the movie screen, like Dorothy in the Wizard of Oz.

One dream she had was about a very large pencil, giant-size, impossible to hold and nearly so to maneuver. She tried to move the pencil so as to write (she had no idea what). She pushed the pencil around with all her strength, falling down and getting up, straining so under the weight of the pencil there was no time or strength or brain cells left to know what to write. This was the most exhausting dream of all, she decided, until the scarecrow dream.

The scarecrow dream was too horrible to utter; she only thought about it and shuddered each time she did, with guilt, and fear, and sorrow. In the dream she was walking up the hill with her mother. It was a sunny day, with hot waves of humidity in front of their eyes, like water to wade through. The girl was encouraging her mother, "C'mon, Mommy, you can do it. Keep going, that's it. That's the way." The mother tried to smile bravely. But there was a problem. Slowly it became obvious the mother wasn't her mother at all. She was a scarecrow. And her straw was falling out everywhere. The girl, horrified but trying to act as if everything was normal, kept picking up the straw, stuffing it into her scarecrow mother's shirt, under her hat, in the back of her pants. Scarecrow was buckling and the girl felt responsible. Wake up! Wake up! She breathed in her surroundings, her bed, her stuffed animals, her school notebooks and pencils. She heard the neighbor boy outside mowing the lawn. Everything is okay, she thought to herself. She luxuriated and sank deep into her bed. Her stomach growled and she thought about Cheerios. A million of them.

Up, Down - Together, Apart

When Sissy turned seventeen, she met Gary. He was her first boyfriend. My sister had trouble all through school. Not having special education was hard for her. Kids made fun of her, and she struggled so much, she was happy to quit in her junior year. Gary was tall and handsome, with disarming blue eyes. But he couldn't read, Mom said. Her girlfriend Amanda dated Gary's brother Max. That's how they met. It wasn't long before my sister was standing down front at the church with Gary, with Rusty performing their wedding ceremony.

When Sissy and Gary got married, Mom and Daddy Sag separated. Mom got a job down at Rockaway Beach on Lake Taneycomo, right near the Arkansas line. Mom and I were a team, buddies, pals. We sang in the car as we wound our way through the curvy Ozark Mountains. Our favorite was Doris Day's "Que Sera, Sera." We sang hymns, too, like "I'll Fly Away" and "The Old Rugged Cross."

I got a job, too. They needed bus boys, and I was eager to get in on the action. At ten years old, I'd be making good money, especially since most days I was on for ten hours, one hour for each year I'd been alive. Johnny Donnini's restaurant was busy all the time. I had my first pizza, first taco, and first fried ravioli there. Mom and I drove back and forth for a while, singing, talking and, for the first time in front of her, smoking. Mom thought I'd get sick after asking for that first puff, but I surprised her. I loved it.

One night on the drive back home it wasn't fun. It was getting dark, and the hairpin curves of the deep Ozark Hills were scary. Mom was upset. I had said something that made her mad and she seemed to not be herself, someone different, unhinged and dangerous. I had never seen her drive like this, fast and careless, her jaw clinched, her eyes squinty and cloudy. I didn't say anything. It wasn't an argument; it was an episode. It wasn't a scolding; it was a whippin', a whippin' of words. I felt small and invisible, gripping the arm that encased the car's door handle. I thought I might accidently open my door, or maybe not accidentally, if she would only slow down. What had come over my sweet mother?

As we raced through the night, the clicking of the bright lights going on and off, on and off, underneath her left foot each time a car came from the opposite direction, I thought we might careen over the railings that girded the steep overhangs of the mountainous curves. I knew we would. I tried closing my eyes but that made it worse. Very quietly, I uttered the words, "Sorry mommy. I'm sorry." This did not help. It made no difference. The speed was overwhelming my thoughts and my words. Mom was yelling about not being appreciated, not being understood. She needed encouragement, not criticism. No one understood how smart she was. She was valedictorian of her graduating class. She could have been a doctor, a lawyer, a congresswoman. She didn't care if she lived or died. She might be better off dead. We all might be. The car screamed across another curve and started down a very steep hill. Would we topple over the hill? I couldn't see the bottom. I prayed for God to help my mommy.

At last, the road calmed down. Familiar gentle slopes were coming into view. I saw the Dairy Queen, the Conoco Station, and the Farmhouse restaurant where Mom used to work. There was no talking now. My breath came easier. As we pulled into the gravel driveway of our house and Mom turned off the car, I put my hand on the door handle and pulled very quietly. As I slipped out of the car I looked up at the bright starry sky, went inside and got into bed.

> *For a long time, this night entered my dreams. I always woke up before the car flipped over going down the steep hill. Another dream was that Mom was driving but also in the back seat. Which one was my mommy? Not the driver, who turned into a monster right before I woke up. Any dream about Mommy I kept deep in my heart. I felt bad that I had the dream, but would never tell her, because she might think I didn't love her. But I loved her more than anything in this world. That's what Mom used to say about her love for me.*

At Rockaway Beach, for a month or so, we stayed in a row of rooms behind the restaurant called the Annex. All the other waitresses were pretty, much younger than mom, but quite a bit older than me. I loved Mom and I was star-struck on the other waitresses. I wanted to be like them. I worked hard and learned how to move fast, do all the jobs: bus tables, run the dishwasher, even take a few items to the customers to help out. Waitresses could stack dishes up their arms and not drop anything, sometimes four or five on one arm. I wanted to do that too and started trying to learn. Johnnie Donnini's son Danny told me I was a hard worker, but I didn't finish things. I started working on that, too.

At 9:00 we'd get off work. That's when the fun began. Johnnie's other son Robbie was my age. We ran all over the place, in and out, playing skee-ball, throwing darts, and the best of them all: the flying cages. Each cage was attached to counter-weighted arms. You got into the cage, standing with no restraints or belts. Inside was a crossbar you held onto in order to move the cage back and forth. The old guy who ran the cages gave everyone a big push to get you going. He smiled and smoked as we pumped away, smiles stretching our faces to the max. Pump, pump, pump, sway, leverage your weight side to side, up and down with your knees and thighs. You could have a partner, which made it easier or harder, depending on your coordination. Robbie and I were often buddies in the cages, and in everything else. Over and over, you went front to back, hoping to make a complete revolution. It was you and the machine. What a thrill to finally get over the hump, feeling the zip of momentum then dropping to just above the ground. Never was a ride more thrilling than the flying cages at Rockaway Beach.

Mom often went bowling with friends after work. She never worried about me, because she said she trusted me. I didn't really understand that, but it sounded good. We used to go to a dark place down some stairs. The people were friendly and always bought me cokes. It was called the Chat 'n Chew. They said, "Howdy, all you friendly friends and neighborly neighbors. Come and smoke and joke and chat and chew!" I loved all the people there and felt they loved me, too. When I turned eleven, they gave me a party, with lots of cake and Coke and even balloons. Much different than my third birthday, I said to myself. My daddy had retreated in my mind and in my life. He seemed to not think of me, and I returned the favor.

After Rockaway Beach, Mom and Daddy Sag decided to give it another go. So, in the fall, it was back to Verona, and the little house on the hill.

It seemed like Gary and Sissy were fighting all the blessed time. He drank a lot, and my sister didn't touch the stuff. He would come home drunk, ready to rumble, and my sister would yell and tell him to get out. When Gary wasn't drinking, he was shy and nervous, but sweet and kind. He smoked Camel cigarettes; his fingers were yellow, and his hands shook. His gorgeous blue eyes were streaked with red lines, like a map to somewhere bad. He could drive, but I don't know how he got his license. I felt safe whenever Gary drove. Once we went to the Dairy Queen and Gary went up to the window and got us all ice cream cones. He brought them out to the car in a cardboard holder. "Here you go," he said with a smile. "Eat it all." "Eat it all" was on the side of the cones. I thought to myself, "Why, Gary can too read." But that might have been all he could read. I asked him to read one of my books to me once and he said no thanks. I liked Gary and wondered why my sister seemed mad at him so much of the time.

Gary's family lived on a farm. On a few occasions, we traveled the fifteen or so miles to visit Sissy when she was first married and living with them. One day Mom and I were driving down to check on my sister. Mom was worried that Sissy was not happy. Sissy was just eighteen and a newlywed. Mom said she thought that Sissy might be pregnant, maybe that was all that was wrong. I thought to myself, wrong? Would that be wrong? They are married, after all.

Mom was wearing her plaid short-sleeve shirt and tan pedal pushers. She had on penny loafers with white anklets and a sun visor that was just the bill of a cap with elastic around her short, curly brown hair. Her left arm was sunburned from resting it outside the car window as she drove. It was sunny and hot as we drove along the old backroads. The sound of wind and the smell of tires on freshly laid blacktop blew through the windows. Mom dug through her purse to find her Rolaids, which she ate pretty much all day, every day, especially when she was nervous. Then she lit a cigarette and it seemed she was all set. But soon she was coughing and tossing her smoke out the window. She pulled a tissue from her pocket, which she always had plenty of, and hacked up some phlegm. It had a streak of blood on it, and Mom showed it to me. I don't know why, except to let someone know that something wasn't right. She dropped the tissue onto the floorboard and said she was better. Except she wasn't. She continued to cough, holding her belly alternately with covering her mouth. I wished I could drive and let her lie down in the back seat. That's what I did whenever I felt bad, and we were in the car. When Mom coughed or moaned or cried out, my stomach hurt, too, and I couldn't be happy till I knew she was okay again. She kept coughing and then started gagging, a sound that was unbearable to me.

"Mommy, Mommy, are you okay?" I asked. She waved her hand to say, "I'm okay, I'm okay." But she couldn't talk anymore.

Suddenly, she pulled to the side of the road, turned off the car, and opened the door. She held onto the steering wheel and stuck her head out, low to the ground. She threw everything up. I closed my eyes tight with each long gasp, followed by retching. I put my hand on her arm and patted. I knew it would end and I hoped it would be soon. In between the retches were the sounds of her voice, moaning, cooing, high and low, asking God to help her. Once she stopped retching, she collected herself. "Ohhh, ohhh, mercy me. Lord have mercy," she said, her voice shaking. She sat up and grabbed another tissue from the endless supply in her pickets to wipe her mouth. Her pretty, deep-set brown eyes were watery and cloudy. She took off her glasses and dabbed them gently. She straightened her shirt, shifted her bosom, and tightened her bra straps. She turned the rearview mirror towards her to check her hair and face. She took a comb to her hair, fished out her compact and powdered her pretty, straight nose. She applied lipstick that she had in her pocket. "Now. That's better, all better now." "Let's sing a song," she said as she started up the car. "How about Que Sera', Sera'?"

I let out a deep sigh and smiled. We sang all the verses of the song. Mom always said, "Que Seda', Seda', like a Spanish speaker. I did it, too. We lingered on the "que' then belted out the "Seda, Seda" like a roller coaster going down a steep hill. "Que Sera,' sera'. Whatever will be will be. The future's not ours to see. Que sera', sera'. What will be will be. The last line was like blue sky to me. It told me not to worry. And when we sang it, I believed what would be, would be good.

Mom took a couple of nerve pills with cold coffee before we went inside the farmhouse. In my sister's bedroom, she told us that she was pregnant-just a few weeks after getting married. Mom acted happy, but looked worried. I was always tuned into her feelings, her facial expressions, and her vibe. Today was no different. Sissy talked a lot about morning sickness and being tired. I hoped everyone would be okay. I asked Sissy if she wanted a boy or a girl. She said she didn't care. I shrugged and spread my hands, "Que sera' sera'!"

While Mom and Sissy talked, I walked outside onto the porch. Gary's father drove the tractor down from the fields around to the muddy circle driveway in front of the big rambling farmhouse with hundreds of rooms, all of them old and musty smelling. I was sitting there, wishing for something to do. So, when asked if I'd like to hop on, I said sure. Mr. Ackerman invited me to stand in front of him on the running boards of his old John Deere. There was plenty of open space to maneuver without fear of collision, so we took off. I was pretty good. Mr. Ackerman put his hands over my flat, nine-year old chest, while I tried to ignore this and concentrate on the practically horizontal steering wheel. It was a strange combination of the thrill of driving and the discomfort of those rough old hands going up and down my front with every bump in the field. I never said anything to anyone about this strange encounter, but I never came close to old man Ackerman again.

Sissy had three kids pretty much back-to-back: La Vonda, my first niece, Patricia Fay, who had cerebral palsy and special needs, and Melanie, a real hellion from the moment she was born. Melanie always wanted to go home with my mom, her grannie. As soon as we started for the car, Melanie would come outside, sit on the ground and start having a tantrum. She cried and screamed till her face was red and she seemed exhausted. She clung to her grannie with desperate strength. My heart always broke to see this, but my sister wouldn't let Mom take one of the kids without taking all of them. This was unreasonable, and the upshot was that the kids didn't come stay with their grannie very much, which was sad. Mom helped Sissy with money and housework when she could. She was still young and tried hard to make sure my sister and her kids were taken care of.

Gary was sweet and shy and likeable when he was sober. His whole demeanor changed, however, after a few beers, and whatever else he might have been drinking. Like one summer evening with a million stars and the crickets singing their hearts out. Sissy called Mom and was breathless. Mom and I came to the rescue. Gary was super drunk. All the doors were open, and the lights were all on. It seemed like the house was inside out. It seemed like the home was blown away in a storm. It seemed like everyone's hair was standing straight out. Gary said really bad things that I had never heard before and hoped to never hear again. Mom hit him on the head with a cast-iron skillet. He lived but soon after this, Sissy and Gary got divorced.

When the car company came and took Mom's car back for non-payment, it was sad, and we cried. The car was a baby blue Ford, shiny and new. That's when we had to get an older, fatter car that wouldn't always start. I knew about jumper cables very early in life. Mom could send me down the road easily enough to a neighbor's house. Ed Start had cables and he was good to us. "Got a minute? Got cables? Our car won't start. Mommy asked if you could give us a jump." "No problem, little lady," he answered. My breath came out like smoke. I always pretended to smoke, like Mom. Winter made this easy.

In summer, if we were traveling, and the car wouldn't start after eating in a restaurant or something, Mom and I had a routine. I would get out of the car, go around to the back and start pushing. We both knew I couldn't do it but other drivers would see us and feel sorry for the little girl trying to push the car so her mom could pop the clutch and get the engine to turn over. It wasn't hard, it was fun, especially in summer.

Daddy Sag had been working construction down in Arkansas and he said things would be better there. It was beautiful and mountainous. The license plates said, "Land of Opportunity" which made me feel kind of happy. What kind of opportunity would we find in Arkansas? Friends, money, happiness and fun? It was a hazy future to gaze into, but I was ready.

The first place we stayed was the Ogden Motel. Tiny green houses, hooked together in an L-shape. It was on the highway with lots of businesses all around. School hadn't quite started so I got to explore a bit. Arkansas' Best Freight (ABF), several little strip malls, restaurants and dry cleaners. All my time with Daddy Sag, people called me Judy Browning, because that was Daddy Sag's last name. My last name was Green, from my own daddy, Emery Green. I was tired of people getting mixed up. So, one day I went to the dry cleaner's and gave them my name: Judy Browning. And it stuck. One little transaction and POOF! I changed my name.

We moved to a trailer park before school started. The trailer was fantastic. Outside it was white, with wooden stairs leading up to the front door. Inside it had wood paneled walls and beautiful blue carpeting. The curtains were orange, matching the blue perfectly, I thought. In the days leading up to school starting – it was just a short walk from the trailer park – I was happy. Mom and Daddy Sag got along well, and I had met a nice neighbor girl with pretty blond hair. Once I had a crick in my neck and her mother helped me brush my hair to get ready for school. At night I washed dishes with the little light on and the rest of the house was dark. The light shone on the bubbles in the sink. The water was warm. The music played on my transistor radio Daddy had given me for Christmas and I felt peaceful and cozy. I liked being alone, washing dishes in the dark.

Sometimes I say something too many times. Maybe I forget that I said it. Maybe I don't remember if I said it to you. Maybe I think I've said it but I'm pretty sure I said it a different way or was making a different point when I said it. That's what happened in school down there in old Fayetteville, Arkansas. Asbell Elementary School. Woodlawn Junior High

School. Apparently, according to some, in their not-so-humble opinions, I talked about my home in Missouri *all the blessed time.* I remembered stuff, compared stuff, explained how a lot of stuff was *better* there than it was here, on and on. I didn't see how I was wrong. I never knew what people thought of it, until they told me in a not-so-friendly way. I was a fish out of water in Arkansas. I was (without knowing it) glued to my hometown of Verona. The *little* hills, the familiar trees and lakes, Roberta, Diana, Carol Sue, even my nemesis, the bullying across-the-street neighbor Maxie. I missed her, too. For a year I struggled. I made mistakes. I got laughed at. I mispronounced Gibraltar (said with hard g and the r in the wrong place: Gil-ba-trar) and got snickered out of the room. I was awkward and shy, yet outspoken and bold, clumsy and lonely, yet funny and goofy, smart and sensitive, yet spacey and clueless. I missed my friends and didn't think I'd ever get used to Arkansas. My teacher Mrs. Thompson would sometimes take me home with her if Mom had to work. I loved staying there and talking with her younger daughter Susan. I was selected to sing Silent Night in German for the school Christmas program, which made me feel proud. At the end of sixth grade, I wrote a poem about Mrs. Thompson. I cried as I read it, and everyone clapped. A boy named Mark with dark hair and a scar over one eye stood up and whistled. That was a truly happy moment. That was a moment I thought I might be at home after all.

New Worlds

It was around this time I started my first diet. Mom took me to the doctor as well as to the dentist. Dr. Rabon gave me the diet to follow, telling me that soon I would be a young woman. I knew I didn't want to be fat, so I followed it faithfully. The battle of the bulge had begun. The war on carbs, the foods that I loved most, was declared. I was in the diet zone, which has lasted most of my life.

In gym class we talked about good nutrition and exercise. The teacher spoke about posture and holding in your stomach, chest up, shoulders back. I said I tried my best, but I still had this problem, pointing to my middle. Your problem is too much ice cream, she said while chuckling. Everyone chuckled with her. My fat has always gathered around my middle. Loose clothing helps and running does, too. Why more teachers didn't take aside their students and counsel them on the necessity and benefit of running is a mystery to me. It was much later in life I discovered the pleasure and the reward from the solitary act of running and walking. Solitude always cleared my head, gave me ideas, and left me feeling better about everything. Schools should have classes in well-being as well as physical exercise. Meditation, quietness, and discussion about self-care and various forms of relaxation seem to me to be critical. It was always on the fringes of the mainstream I encountered this wisdom. I hope for a time when these conversations move much more to the forefront of education. I see some evidence of it in places and wonder about the results, which should be more harmony and healthy relationships with one's own body and with others.

The girls talked about their periods a lot. I was alone quite a bit, with mom working all the time. I listened to music and danced and wondered, *when will my period come?* Once while looking at greeting cards, waiting for mom to get off work, something weird happened. Standing right there in the drugstore, in front of birthday cards for moms and daughters, I wet my pants. Without any warning, it started, and the pee just kept coming, right down into my bobby socks. Mom was waiting in the car when I walked out, and I told her about it. She looked worried but didn't say anything. The next day it happened. My period came with some nasty cramps. I was so happy! Not because I liked cramps, but because I was becoming a young woman, just like the good doc said.

Summer came and with it a whole new adventure. On the other end of the trailer park lived a tall, older, handsome boy, with green eyes, an elegant nose and a generous mouth and jawline. His black hair was cropped short with a stylish little bit of length on top, somewhere between a flat top and a crew cut. Billy was eighteen and six-feet tall. He swaggered when he walked. He was funny, confident and made my body come alive in private places. At night we met and talked and laughed. When he first kissed me, I thought I might gag. I had never heard of anyone kissing like that! I pushed him away and ran to the trailer. I told my mom later that he made me feel funny. He made me tickle "down there." She smiled. I didn't know anything. I knew I liked Billy, but that kissing was too much. No more kissing like that, for sure! Shortly after making this clear to Billy on our walks around the park, he pulled me to him very gently, very slowly. He kissed softly and gentlemanly and I relaxed. We kissed some more, and it wasn't long before I got the hang of the pleasure of Billy's kind of kissing.

We were together every night. We kissed and made out hot and heavy. Billy thought I was 15 and when he discovered I was 13, it kind of broke his heart. He never went too far but it would have been so easy for both of us. One night he said, "Three years. That's all I'll wait. Then we have to get married." Whoa, I thought. What about what *I* want? I never said anything, but I let Billy think I'd wait three years with him for about a month.

We moved to a different trailer park. Near a cliff, on the side of a hill were descending rows and rows of trailers. Singles, doublewides, over-sized RVs, and cute ones like ours. Trailer living was different. No yards to mow, not many neighbors to get to know, because no one walks, they just drive, and their attention is on where they're going. After Billy, there was Ernie, then Bobby, then a slew of co-workers and just friends that were fun to talk to but that was about it.

At the bottom of the long hill with all the trailers, was Cliff's Drive-in. I walked in one day, said I was looking for work, and they hired me on the spot. A girl named Terry advised me on the job. "Just go up, say hi, flirt a little." "How do you flirt?" I wanted to know. Then it was my turn to take a customer. I smiled, said hi, and took the order. When I got back Terry laughed, "How do you flirt? Yeah, right."

I loved working. Working for me was a dance, an outlet, the chance to forget any troubles or worries. I loved working the intercom, experimenting with my voice, being busy and making tips. We wore a coin changer that hung on our short black aprons called a caddy. Pennies,

Julie G. Olmsted

nickels, dimes and quarters. Pockets on the aprons held the dollar bills. Learning to make change was fun and something few seem to know now, in the age of computerized everything. Let's say the bill was $10.71. How do you make change from a twenty? You count up. 71+4 pennies to 75 cents. A quarter makes a dollar, or eleven. Four singles make it fifteen. Plus, a five takes it up to twenty. There's your change, Bub. Super fun for a thirteen-year-old smarty pants.

Opal

I met someone who worked in the kitchen named Opal. Opal was short and strong, with salt and pepper hair that curled softly around her face. She wore glasses attached to a delicate chain with tiny pearls. She had an ample bosom, over which she wore a white cook's apron, doubled up in the middle to compensate for her height. Opal had an olive complexion and a straight mouth, seemingly always tightly closed, except for sometimes, when she would speak only what was necessary to get the job done. She was no-nonsense.

I was an emotional, pubescent, smart mouth, with boundless energy and a less than healthy regard for "the rules." But I loved working and turns out I loved cleaning too, and maybe that was the meeting place for the likes of Opal and me. Our friendship certainly didn't happen overnight. It was several months in the making. And it had its turnaround in the surprising occurrence of a single line uttered by Opal on a very busy and hectic Saturday night. Opal turned to me and simply said, "I don't like you."

No one had ever said that to me before. Opal's comment was not uttered with meanness or anger. There was no request to "iron everything out" or reasons why she was right about her opinion. It was simply the way Opal felt and she apparently thought I should know it. What to do? Well, I was so stunned that I said nothing. And we were too busy to engage in an out and out discussion about the matter. I remember the comment stinging a bit. Probably my mouth dropped open in youthful disbelief and surprise. Maybe my eyes registered hurt or a flash of momentary anger. I seemed to understand that there was nothing to say in response to this little arrow to my heart. But I also knew that I needed to keep working. There were orders to take, trays to deliver and hang on car windows, money to be collected and change to be made.

So, I kept working. As did Opal. Nothing further was said. Not that night nor in the days that followed. What can you do when a person says simply, "I don't like you?" Not a whole lot, it turns out. It felt like a slap in the face. No one likes to be told this, and very few receive this kind of direct communication. But I knew Opal was honest. She worked hard and she never gossiped. She didn't laugh much, but so what? While I was twirling and laughing and flirting and working hard, too, maybe Opal saw something in me that was missing in her. Or maybe she saw something in me that she grew up being told was wrong or unattractive or even offensive. And she had the right to dislike it. Even at age thirteen I knew this. I couldn't talk her into liking me. I couldn't argue that I was, indeed, likeable, adorable, even. I couldn't say how much my mother loved me, and I couldn't whisper to her how Billy had stolen a kiss from me and told me he was going to marry me once I turned sixteen. I couldn't show her my pretty clothes and new record player, or sing to her or flatter her or anything like that to convince her that she ought to like me. So, there it lay. Opal didn't like me. Did I like her? Yes, if I was honest, I did.

I let it go. I said nothing about it ever. But in the days that followed, something strange began to happen. Opal began to smile more. Had I not noticed this before or was it something new? What I did know that certainly *was* different was that her smile found its focus in my direction from time to time. Opal seemed to lighten up a bit. I smiled back at her, once I began to trust that she was no longer apt to bite my head off for some unexpected and shocking reason. Opal was a straight shooter. She would never have done that, I came to realize. And, over time, maybe a period of a few months, Opal and I became chums. She laughed and her eyes twinkled. She helped me when I needed it. And when I left Cliff's to go back to Missouri, Opal hugged me good-bye.

Happy and Gay

Markie worked at Cliff's, too. Markie was short and stocky, strong and mean-looking. Her hair was short, dark and often oily. She had a sprinkling of freckles on her face and always wore a black tee-shirt and blue jeans. She had a couple of decayed front teeth, between which was almost always a toothpick. Markie's eyes kind of smoldered but twinkled when she laughed. She laughed at things I said a lot. I was dumb in the ways of the world; Markie knew this, and it amused her. She sidled up to me in a way that made me kind of nervous. She put her arm around me, and I became squeamish. Then she would get mad. "You think I'm some kind of pervert!" she would say to me angrily. I didn't know what a pervert was, but I didn't think Markie was one, at least I didn't think I thought that. "No, I don't!" I would respond.

Markie was what my mom called a "lesbin." She was (in Mom's words) "mannish." But that didn't matter to me. I loved Markie because she was protective of me. She thought things that I said were funny but were actually just dumb and she accompanied me to parties that I probably shouldn't go to. Once we went to a party and I saw a man with no pants on. I was shocked but tried not to show it. Later I said, "I thought they were that big!" showing my hands held apart about a foot. Markie laughed her head off. A little while later she tried to kiss me, and I forbade it. We pretty much stopped hanging out after that.

I worked at Cliff's Drive-In Monday through Thursday and picked up another job at a drive-in called Vic-Mon Friday through Sunday. I gave all my earnings to Mom. Daddy Sag found a job somewhere in Louisiana, driving a truck. He wasn't around much, and Mom worked a lot, too. I had a problem in school. I kept falling asleep. I went to the school counselor once after slapping someone named Melly in the lunch line. Melly made a smart remark about my hair, and I just slapped her. My counselor told me I used a rifle when a bb gun would work better. After this, Mrs. Hileman hired me to work for her an hour every day and let me nap. I always appreciated her advice about a bb gun. But for a long time I continued to use a rifle.

School was never as interesting to me as work. I was constantly worried about my acceptance and my looks. I could never make my hair do like the cheerleaders' hair, but it wasn't for not trying. I went to a salon and described what I wanted: "It's straight and it swings. It's real shiny and curves around my cheeks like this." The hairdresser tried, too. But it just wouldn't cooperate, my hair. It was hopelessly wavy and went in weird directions. In the mornings I brushed my hair, drew it up on one side and put a big bow in it. I thought it looked nice but then I saw the cheerleaders' hair and changed my mind. I was shy and felt invisible. I had a friend for a summer named Susie. She lived in the same trailer park as me. Susie and I had lots of fun until school started. We said we were best friends, in fact. But she started running around with a bunch of girls who didn't seem to like me. I sat up in the top bleachers at a ball game once and called down to Susie, who was sitting with the other girls close to the action. When she looked up, I said, "Still best friends?" Susie looked at me with pity and shook her head no. I was stupid like that in school. Just asking to be kicked in the gut.

Work was always fun. I was never afraid to do anything, carhop, take orders on the intercom, cook, or clean. I always filled in whenever asked. It never bothered me to come in early or stay late. I often worked double shifts. At school I was bored and tired. At work I was the eager beaver.

Harriet had straight, short, black hair, freckles and a slight bump on her nose. Her cheeks were rosy, and she loved to act goofy. This was our friendship nexus. We laughed and made fun of everything, including ourselves. Harriet was also friends with Susie, but she kept our friendship separate. Most of the time I hung out with Muriel, who was heavy and pretty and soft-spoken and kind. Muriel laughed at all my jokes and went with me everywhere. I thanked God for her and when we moved back to Missouri where I belonged, Muriel held me close and sobbed.

Pulling Away

I continued to visit Daddy and Marge occasionally. They had moved to Mesa, Arizona, a suburb of Phoenix. I thought I might go live with them. I thought this because it seemed to me that my mom was not well. I didn't know in what way, exactly. I just knew I felt unsafe somehow. I couldn't say out loud what I was feeling because it would be a betrayal to my mom. Later I could see that I was struggling to preserve my own mental equilibrium. Her consumption of Rolaids, nerve pills, beer and caffeine, seemed natural to me, until it didn't. She never stopped working. She always came home. But there was an increasing instability that called me to do something that felt risky but necessary. I thought that I might be doing myself some good by making this move. I didn't think I had any other option.

I left in winter. Mom hugged me close as I was about to board the big Greyhound. The white breath coming from our mouths mingled with the roar of engines, the smell of exhaust, happy reunions and tearful good-byes. Busses departing and arriving cut through our conversation. "Now, you listen to me," she said. "You're mine, and don't you forget it." She said this through clenched teeth and with some humor, but it made me feel confused and a little more nervous than I already was. *How could I leave my mom? What would she do without me?* I stepped up, looked out the window and waved. I pointed at me, crossed my arms over my chest, then pointed at her. When would I return? Why was I even going?

Back at Cliff's Drive-in, Cliff's adult son had brought in a bunch of sweatshirts with the logo on the back. On the front of some was the picture of a little devil with a pitchfork. It said across the top, "I'm a horny little devil." That's the one I got. It was bright orange. Not knowing what a horny little devil was, I put on my sweatshirt one chilly morning at Marge and Daddy's house. Daddy never had to be harsh with me or punish me in any way for things I did. All he had to do was what he did when he saw my sweatshirt. "Now that will never go around here." His eyes were disapproving. His tone was somber. I was heartbroken. I ran to my room and cried in shame. But I didn't know what the shame was about. It was the same shame I thought might get rid of if I went to confession. It was dark and it hurt in my whole body. Daddy followed me into the room and sat on the bed. "Now you know we can't go without locking horns once in a while." Was Daddy a horny devil, too? Why didn't I ask him what the sweatshirt meant? Why didn't I tell him that I didn't know? Because I was mute. Words failed me. I wanted to tell Daddy so many things. I wanted him to know that I knew now what he meant years before when he said Mom was "too much." I blurted out an attempt, "Mom is not, she can't, she's just…"

But I could never say it. I thought my mom was mentally unstable. I wanted to tell Daddy so he might understand. What I didn't know was that this suspicion on my part about Mom was the lynchpin of the whole divorce debacle. They never worked things out. She thought he was unfaithful. He thought she was unstable.

There was truth to both sides. But unshared hurt and misunderstanding that is never cleared up is the foundation of a lifetime of bitterness. Daddy could never have understood what I was trying to say with any compassion for my mom. Maybe for me, but never her. And that was a barrier for my sharing my own anguish. It takes courage to hear unwelcome news that might have something to do with you. Daddy never had this courage. It took me a long time to see it, but years later, I finally did. My years-long heartbreak about my parents was not that they got divorced. It was that they never achieved a peaceful settlement and became friends. This is the destructive power of divorce, never growing up and forgiving one another. I believe my mom finally achieved this. Daddy never did.

School in Arizona was a strange place for me. The hallways were outside, like a motel. I made no friends. I said I was sick a lot. Daddy would say to me, "Just go. If you still feel bad later in the day, you can always call." I would go. I would stay. My teacher called Daddy and Marge to say that my penmanship was bad. Daddy spoke sternly to me. I tried hard to improve, but never got far. How could they focus on the quality of my penmanship when my whole world was off kilter? My penmanship no doubt showed this. But, oh well. Just keep trying to improve. This became an exhausting theme of my life.

Marge complained that I washed my hair too much. Being a beautician, she told me, "Washing every day is not good for your hair." I explained, "I'm not washing it every day. I'm just wetting it to roll it up." She didn't believe me. I showed her the shampoo bottle. She looked away. There were some good times. I had to be reminded to dry the silverware every night. I always forgot. "Would you remind me when I get married to dry the silverware?" This was to my stepsister Sherry and Margie. They laughed and promised to remind me.

Pulling Away

Chip was my half-brother. That means we had the same dad but not the same mom. People often were confused when I tried to explain all the halves and wholes and steps in the family. It was my little tutorial that helped them understand. They always laughed at how I told it. Once a friend of my dad's told me I should take my show on the road.

My half-brother Chip was annoying me one day and I shot out after him. Marge stepped in and told me I had a murderous look on my face. She said I looked like my mother. I said there's nothing wrong with my mother. That's when Marge crossed the line. "Your mother's a barfly." Another word I didn't know. But I knew it wasn't good. I pictured a fly with a big head, like the movie I had seen with Sissy, sitting up at a bar. I saw red and lunged at my stepmother. I wanted to hurt her for saying such a thing. She screamed and ran. She ran like I was a monster, which made me even madder.

She called my dad at the body shop where he worked all day. She said she was going to calm herself down by doing some sewing. Daddy came home and came into the bedroom where I was miserable and crying. When I tried to tell him again that my mom wasn't well, he told me a story. The story was about someone who was drowning, and another person tried to help him but had to walk away because he was going to drown too, if he kept trying to help. This story I knew was about my mom, but I didn't really know how to respond to the story. It made me very sad to think about my mom drowning. I knew I would do anything to make sure that didn't happen. Anything. Then we got down to brass tacks about what to do next. Everyone became a little cheerful after all agreed that I would take my first airplane ride back home to my mom the upcoming week. I was going home again. To my drowning mother.

Mom continued to wrestle with her demons. She felt sick sometimes after a meal and would just go to the bathroom and stick her finger down her throat to help her throw up and feel better. I believe this was because she ate too fast, and often, too much. I know this because it has been my lifelong struggle, too. It might have been due to nerves, but also to being a waitress for so long and never having the time to sit and eat a leisurely meal. She was always on the move, never stopping for long. Her ulcers went away after she finally stopped working. The smoking stopped too, but not before the cough became permanent and her steps became slow and few, due to COPD, which eventually took her life.

Julie G. Olmsted

Driving was a huge deal to most of us in rural Missouri. Over time I found that driving was a fine way to calm down, enjoy the view, and even feel at peace. I took Driver's Education at Verona high school, of course. Forrest Weaver was our instructor, who also happened to be the biology teacher and basketball coach, strictly for boys. Mr. Weaver was a bit rough and sarcastic. But he was a good Driver's Ed. instructor. On the road I felt happy and free. The speed limit out on Highway 60 was 70MPH. I reached that limit within seconds of taking the wheel. "THE SPEED LIMIT IS ONLY FOR IDEAL DRIVING CONDITIONS!!" was always his admonition when hitting my stride at about 69MPH. I knew I had to slow down then, which I did. It wasn't my car; it was the school's. I wasn't alone on the open road; I had passengers. "Your passengers have to feel safe," was another maxim he used frequently, and one I still try to obey. I passed the class with flying colors.

I feel bad that young people no longer get to take Drivers' Ed in high school. Driving school is very expensive and the lessons are a solitary experience, whereas it's fun to jump in the car with two or three other nerds like you. I suppose insurance is a concern, like when is it not nowadays? I am grateful for the experience I had as a young person in high school, as fraught as it was with disappointment and grief about what was going on at home. I am especially grateful for teachers who cared and extended a kind hand and a listening ear. Public school teachers are unrecognized angels. They need much more freedom, respect, and compensation. We give teachers our children for a huge chunk of the day. They deserve to be seen as partners in creating the future for us all. They deserve to be listened to and given the benefit of the doubt with their observations about our children.

Leaving Again

I tried to leave Mom again when I turned fifteen. We were fighting, fighting. I couldn't relax at home. Like her, I was always on the go. She was nearly always out with her new boyfriend Gordon, coming home drunk, losing her temper, keeping me awake. We weren't buddies now. It felt like we were enemies. Daddy said I could come live with him if I wanted.

I left because I thought I needed to. I left because I felt unsafe, confused and unmoored. I left because I was lost at home.

In Oklahoma you could get your permit to drive with another licensed driver at age 15. That was a definite perk living for a time down in Miami, Oklahoma with Daddy after Marge died. She died of a heart attack and had spoken to my mom on the phone the day before. So, of course Daddy blamed Mom for her death, which he mentioned to me several times. I never responded but took note. Inside, I hated my dad for blaming my mom for his wife's death. It wasn't fair to blame her. But as usual, I couldn't say anything. If I did, he might get stern with me. And I would start crying. And he would say what he always said, "I should have shot myself a long time ago." This made me feel terrible and made sure that I almost never brought up anything too upsetting. Daddy needed to feel he was on an even keel.

He had a big re-built 1960 Ford Pickup truck that was mean and sweet and a blast to drive. It was a five-speed stick shift that I adjusted to easily, although once I thought it would be a good idea to downshift while going 50MPH on the highway. Daddy yelled just in time and set me straight on downshifting at high speeds. I didn't bother to tell him about the Dodge adventure. He told me with tears in his eyes one day, that he wasn't "equipped" to take care of me. He was sorry, but I would have to go back to Mom's, which I was ready to do anyway.

I had to go back because I was too much, too. I had to go back because there was no home for me here. I had to go back and try to feel at home, at home.

Wheels of Fun

Mom would often let me drive in rural settings. Nearly every setting was rural where we lived, so I drove quite a bit. I complained occasionally about all the cars we had being "fat." "When are we ever going to get a skinny car?" I would whine. Once, in a fat, old blue Plymouth 1950 Special Deluxe, I took a few friends for a joy ride. On the way down the hill from our house, the brakes failed. Pump, pump, pump, nothing. Of course it was a stick shift, so instinctively I began to downshift, but only toward the bottom of the hill, knowing that to strip the gears was to say good-bye to Old Blue. Third to second, no one coming from either direction at the foot of the hill by the Baptist church, whew. Continuing up the smaller hill, I kept pumping the brake, but as the car slowed, we all started to breathe a bit easier, and by the time we were downtown I was able to pull back the shifter to first gear, which ended the spontaneous and unintended coaster ride. My friends all applauded me. I was a hero and a genius, apparently, an accolade with which I didn't care to disagree. The groundwork of my self-acclaimed driving prowess had been laid.

The big day came finally, when I went to get my license. Was there anything more exciting than getting your license two days after your sixteenth birthday? Our old Rambler with one seat in the front was not only not passable, but not available either. I had been semi-dating a guy named Tim Alcott, who had a super sweet 1968 Dodge Charger, dark green with a black vinyl top. Every boyfriend I had needed to let me drive his car, a prerequisite for anything pleasant or lasting in the relationship. I wasn't serious about Tim, but he was nice and decent looking. His car, however, was a driver's dream. I thought about it, then I asked, would Tim let me borrow his car for my Driver's Test? Why, yes, he would. Tim's car had black interior, a smooth looking console down the middle of the newly issued "bucket seats," which were not good for dating or late-night parking, but very good looking, and an automatic transmission, *so* easy to maneuver. I passed of course, and cruised down Main Street where Tim was waiting to go for a breezy, fun-filled ride through the Ozark Hills, music blaring and unknown pleasures in the evening that lay ahead.

My future short-term husband Herm taught me that driving was an art, not just something that got you from one place to another. He schooled me on steadiness, focus, passing and tailgating. I loved driving so his instruction was welcome. I was a rapt student and gained confidence with his tutelage. Once a mutual friend of ours gave me such a compliment on my driving. He said, "You should come drive trucks for us, Judy. You drive like a pro." Herman smiled outside, and I glowed inside. I felt a little like one of the boys, which was always a secret goal. It was a goal to be seen and respected, like they seemed to see and respect each other. Herm's teaching stuck with me throughout life. In one of my first conversations with my future long-term husband I told him, "I can drive anything." He loved that comment and referred to it many times over the years.

Those Lucky People

I always loved learning, tests, sentence dictation, even Math, which we called arithmetic until fifth grade. Spelling was so easy I wondered why we did it. I knew there were people who struggled with school. There was Larry, who couldn't stay in his seat. There was Billy B., and Steve T., who spoke in ways you could barely understand. Billy was what we called a greaser. He combed his hair back with some kind of oil, maybe his own, but I would never say that about him or to him. He had a few pieces that stood up on top, and his face was freckled. If I gave Billy a nickname it might have been Dancer, like my pet rooster that Daddy Sag served for Sunday dinner. He appeared a bit like a rooster with no feathers, someone who looked like he might crow any minute, not too appealing but very cute and endearing. I gravitated toward the smart ones, those who might be kind of invisible, like I usually felt. We had many brainy conversations that I couldn't have at home, or even with my girlfriends. We laughed, smoked, fought and made up. But, with Carol Sue I could have any conversation. Sometimes it felt like we were the same person. Once, as college students, we took mescaline together. For a few moments we actually echoed each other's every word. Carol Sue was the best of who I really wanted to be. In high school, in class, we were virtually inseparable. Things didn't bother her like they did me. She didn't try to be liked. She was above all that.

Carol Sue and I would sit together in class. In high school she was pissed off that our English teacher Mrs. Fields rarely even showed up to teach. She started a calendar, marking the days she came and the days she didn't. We attended a school board meeting and showed the calendar to those in attendance. Mrs. Fields eventually retired. She was the wife of the superintendent and we later suspected she was kept on for that reason. Because at some point, we all became aware of Mrs. Field's alcoholism and resulting fragility that caused her chronic absenteeism. She should have gotten help. Someone should have stood up for the learning of the students. This was harmful leniency. But we were just teenagers. What did we know?

At senior prom we went together, unescorted by the requisite male. Although we were friends with James and John and had some flirtations with Danny and Billy and had pleasant exchanges with Eldon and Steve, no one dared come near us to ask us for a date. Or that is how it looked.

Those Lucky People

We went outside the set parameters of boy/girl offerings of a small rural high school. We liked Aurora boys, or Monett boys. These were the towns we typically drove back and forth to on a Friday or Saturday night. Carol had a dark blue Chevy Malibu, stick shift, with a black vinyl top. Her parents owned the local telephone company and were well respected in the town, while I kind of came from the wrong side. That is, Mom was Daddy Sag's third wife, and he was her third husband. She was a waitress; he was a truck driver and construction worker. For a time, they managed the local tavern in Verona. And you might think that would put them on par with Carol Sue's dad, who, as far as I know, was sitting at that tavern every blessed night of his life, except when they were all on a very special family vacation, like to Washington D.C. or the Grand Canyon, places I could only dream about. Red, Carol's dad as he was called, got falling-down drunk…a lot. But he did own the telephone company. And he did take his family on great educational vacations. So, I suppose that made him some kind of big shot in the community. My folks knew their place and I knew mine. And that's why I thought I was lucky to have Carol as my best friend.

Carol Sue and I went everywhere we wanted in that Chevy. On Prom Night we decided to go beyond Monett and Aurora, all the way into Springfield. We met a friendly older black guy who we took riding around with us. We were so carefree, we laughed and smoked and asked if we could touch his hair, which he didn't mind at all. Something bad might have happened that night but it all turned out great. We had so many great nights. When I moved away from home at sixteen, Carol helped me. She picked me up from home in Monett, nine miles away. She took me to school and to work at Lakeland Restaurant every night at five in the evening. We drove up and down Main St., in Monett, in Verona and Aurora. Once, just for fun, she, Berta, Di and I drove around the Dairy Twist one hundred and one times, non-stop, with the radio blaring, of course. We smoked Marlboro cigarettes, French inhaling with great flare. We drank on the weekends. We laughed our heads off. On the rare occasion when my mom expressed worry about me, I always reassured her that I had a guardian angel. When it came to the night life, I was never afraid.

Julie G. Olmsted

Carol Sue, Senior Pics, 1970

One of the places we went fairly often in summer was Table Rock Lake. Carol Sue's family had a boat on Big M Boat Dock, and she could drive the boat, no problem. When Berta and Di's family went to their cabin on the lake, we would all go water-skiing. I learned to love skiing and got pretty good at it. Carol was excellent.

We roomed together our first year of college, at Southwest Missouri State in Springfield. That first year I was ecstatic. I discovered I had discipline, too, because I was intensely interested in every class I took. I realized part of my problem in high school was that it was not challenging. But now things were different. On my own I had a better, stronger sense of myself, somewhat detached from the image of "poor girl from the wrong side of town." Carol and I still went home for the weekends, continuing in our tradition of cruising, drinking, and experimenting with boys. One day she got a call. It was her mother. Massive heart attack. Don't know if she'll make it. Come home now.

We used to get up early to study, sometimes 4:30 or 5. I never dropped this habit, and early rising is automatic now, which has its benefits and downsides, the main one being you can't stay up late easily. This day, we had gotten up that early and headed the forty miles or so to her home to be with her dad and big sister and two brothers that evening when she got the call. I don't know why I was with her, except to say that

Those Lucky People

I was almost always with her. That day we were up twenty-four hours, which wasn't all that unusual back then; it's just I remember her saying, "Hey, Jude, we've been up twenty-four hours." She could still say that after losing her mom.

She moved back home to care for her dad and brothers. Her older sister, Mary, was mentally unstable and could not be counted on to do the household chores that her mother once did. Carol could cook and clean and study and go out with boys and never seem to miss a beat. I used to sit and watch her dry her hair with the window fan, admiring her hair and her strength and her righteousness. I felt a great loss when she went back home to live. I tried to be helpful, but it seemed my help was so incidental; Carol Sue was that self-sufficient, or so I thought.

I learned about the longest day of the year while driving in the car with Carol Sue. We often commented that the sky was the color of Easter eggs. We were free and wild and drunk with youth and the beauty that surrounded us. We drove to the lake, jumped into the water and then watched the stars come out while lying on the hood of her Chevy Malibu, passing a bottle of rum back and forth, contemplating infinity; that's what we called it.

Once, driving down to the lake there was magic blowing through the car windows. It was a breathtaking Ozark Mountain summer's day, with skies the color of Robin eggs and trees bursting with green that poured beauty in all directions. The wind whipped our hair across our eyes, the radio blared, "Bye-bye Miss American Pie." We knew all the words and belted them out full tilt. We sailed through the hills, taking the hairpin curves without a concern. Carol had a keen sense of direction, and she was a great driver. We headed for the boat dock and pulled onto the soft sand of the small beach surrounding the dock. In silence, we opened our doors and kicked off our shoes, feeling the warm welcome of the sand. And we started to laugh. What's funny? I remember thinking. But I couldn't stop, and neither could she. We weren't laughing at anything at all. We were allowing the joy that was deeply and naturally in us to escape. It was a holy experience, a gift of grace from the ancient and always new. We were touching and knowing Emmanuel, *God with Us*, fully and intimately. We laughed and gasped and cried, each one pointing to the other: "You're weird," we both were saying, and laughing more until we fell down in the sand, pointing, chuckling, tears streaming. Silence now. Then we did something very strange, even for us. In our innocence and pure love, we embraced and tenderly kissed.

Julie G. Olmsted

Carol got a call from someone not quite a year later, saying her father had been in an accident. Seemed he decided to drive himself home from the tavern. Often someone would offer him a ride and he would accept, but not this night. It was quick. No suffering. Instantaneous. Gone.

Carol Sue was stoic. Her brothers, too, seemed to bear up in a way that was both puzzling and inspiring to me. We were now not so very close, she and I. She had a boyfriend with whom she was living. She dropped out of college and got on with her life. I continued with my dramas back in Southern Missouri. One day out of the blue, I got a phone call that Carol wanted to see me. She was in a hospital in Philadelphia, having gotten married to someone in that area and given birth to three children, one boy and a set of twin girls. But she was sick now. It was cancer. Could I come, just this once?

The last time I saw her was in the hospital visiting area. The sun was shining through the dirty windows where we sat. We had light conversation in which we laughed some, cried a little. She told me she wanted to touch my cheek, and I said, "Go ahead."

"You will forever be in my heart," I gave a little sob. "I know," she responded. "I love you."

"And I love you."

Not long after she left the world, Carol Sue's eldest brother Ron died in a forest fire. Her other older brother died, too, somehow. Her sister Mary moved to a nursing home and her younger brother works construction close to where we grew up. I am grateful that this lucky, rather well to do family took all those fancy vacations together. In my sorrow for my friend, I am grateful too, to have known and loved her. But in the spring of the year, when the sky turns Easter Egg blue and pink, I still miss her.

Work as a Refuge

I started working at Lakeland Restaurant in Monett my junior year of high school. Monett was nine miles from our town, Verona, and the point at which you turned south to go to Table Rock Lake, near Branson. I worked from 5 to 10pm during the week, 12-8pm on the weekends, unless they needed someone to work a double, which was 6-2 then 2-10pm, which I did often. Why not? I was young, energetic and truly loved being a waitress. I loved the spin. The spin was when you got so busy, twirling and serving, dancing through customers, tables, back and forth through the swinging door to the kitchen, opening/shutting the oven warmer, where homemade breads and cinnamon rolls kept their tender warmth, listening to the radio in the kitchen play all the hits of the day (think Simon & Garfunkel, Herman's Hermits, the Beatles), out to the cool, elegant dining room where "piped in" elevator music played softly to hungry, happy people. I loved movement, coordination, doing several things at once, having everything come out on time. Now and then I'd work the grill and the amazing "Broasted Chicken" fryer. I especially liked filling in for the breakfast short order cook, Dale. Breakfasts were a super-fast and demanding gig. I routinely felt myself high and giddy, whether working the grill or serving customers. Working I always felt useful, focused and upbeat. Moving from one task to another absorbed my thoughts and gave me energy I could count on.

People in my immediate family have shown themselves to be perfectly happy sitting and watching television all day. My sister, you could argue, eventually died of sitting. She sat so much one day she just couldn't get up. This is a fate I pray to avoid. I feel I owe much of this attitude to my bosses at Lakeland restaurant, Van and Eleanor. And, of course, Jack Lalanne. My mom had worked at Lakeland before I did. There was some story I never got the full scoop on about her being fired. I never asked for details and mom never offered, probably a good thing. On those days when business was slow, we cleaned. The milk machine, with its long rubber mini hoses extending from the huge plastic bags of milk needed to be kept spotless, as did the area behind the milk bags. The shelves containing salt, pepper, sugar, napkins and silverware had to be rid of any dust or crumbs, washed in hot water and vinegar, dried and shined to perfection. When doing what was called "side work" salt and pepper shakers were filled, wiped and shined on top. This was done with alacrity and discretion, never as a drudgery or without the touch of a pro. Small towels were used to clean tables and booths, dipped in hot vinegar water, handily wrung out and folded neatly to do the job. These were called "counter cloths," never *ever* rags. That was much too indelicate for a beautiful, elegant restaurant like Lakeland. Every time you cleaned a table, salt and pepper shakers, napkin holders and ash trays were cleaned, as well as the area underneath them. I made sure that these items were set properly distanced from the wall and each other, a small tableau, of sorts. Tables were wiped with precision with the neatly folded counter cloths, as well as the edges around the table. After that (never before, because crumbs often fell to the seats if you couldn't catch them all with your hand), you wiped out the booths. We were taught to make sure that the booths nor the tables were to be wet when a customer was seated. If it required a dry cloth or napkin to wipe up extra droplets, you took care of that. Napkin holders were never to be filled too full, as that caused customers to have to tug and pull, inconveniencing them, as well as pulling out way too many napkins, which was wasteful.

This was all in the coffee shop. Beyond the coffee shop was the dining room. The dining room was usually closed until the weekends. There was an atmosphere of refinement in the dining room. Eleanor (Mrs. Van to us young waitresses) was very creative, especially with candles and Christmas trees. She had a way of melting various candles over green wine bottles that made them look like waterfalls. I couldn't imagine how she did it then and can't now. But when you gazed out over the vast dining room, those candles shining softly, illuminating the cascading wax waterfalls, it was breathtaking. She also knew how to manage what was called angel hair. Several trees graced the restaurant at Christmastime, all elaborately decorated with a million lights, then covered with gauzy angel hair (delicate and potentially dangerous spun glass), creating a magical effect I don't recall seeing anywhere else in all my life. I was proud to be a part of the Lakeland crew.

Our dress and grooming were a star condition of our employment. Starting with the hair, most of us had long hair, the young ones that is. Pulled up to a neat bun set right at the crown, not on top, neither a ponytail or low bun, nice and high, full and not a hair out of place. Except the little curls on the side. These were pin curls, set with bobby pins an hour or so before work and sprayed. Right before leaving the house, I'd take out the bobby pins, pull down the curls, carefully comb them to a perfect S-curve, then spray again. All set, but for make-up, which was perfect, down to the mascara, separating the lashes with a straight pin for precision.

Dresses were snowy white, zipped up the front, topped with spotless shiny black aprons. Silky, nude colored hose were neatly clipped with garter belts, later to be replaced with the blessed pantyhose, which provided support, comfort and smoothness to the whole look. Never, no never, a run in those panty hose, or risk being sent home as a consequence. Then there were the clinic shoes. Tennis shoes? Horror! Sneakers, loafers, casual slip-ons? Absolutely not. Comfortable, supportive (and I thought, somewhat sexy) lace up white clinic shoes, polished and shined nightly. I learned this ritual shoe shining with Mom's clinic shoes. Each time I went to work, my presentation was a work of art. I twirled in the mirror, checking every detail. Voila! I was ready to meet my public. I was on top of my game.

It paid off to pay such attention to detail, both in my look and in my service. I learned to anticipate my customers' every need. I thoroughly enjoyed bringing extras to the table before they were requested, especially if children were present. Coffee pouring with a flair and great enthusiasm for extra trips (Certainly, be right there, my pleasure, anything else I can get for you?) were my oft-said quips. I was paid fifty-three cents an hour for my work, frequently forgetting to pick up my check, since I made good tips, lots of "crispies," as we called the coveted dollar bills left under a plate. I paid for all my clothes, food and fun with my tips. In my junior year I started putting most everything in a piggy bank, which I filled again and again, then emptied and rolled for the regular bank for college.

Working was my passion, my pastime, my passport to independence. It was also my lifeline. Through working, I was freed from home, freed from worry, about my sister, my mother, my future or anything else. I loved being tired, being spent, having achy feet and legs. Mom would sometimes rub my feet when I got home from work. You haven't lived until you have an expert foot rub with – are you ready – rubbing alcohol. Oh man, what a feeling! Life was always good after a day of hard work.

Boys and Booze

The most exciting thing in life, for what seemed like a very long time, was boys. Boys. Beautiful, muscular, strutting, winking, funny, rude, handsome, hot, smart-ass boys. I wanted to be close to them, to smell them, touch them, maybe even be them, a little. Whenever two or more of them gathered, there was bragging, of course, but mostly laughter. They made each other laugh a lot. I noticed something interesting in the early years of my life with boys. Whenever I chimed in with my own brand of wit and charm, boys would often groan and do the eyeroll. I knew that what I said was just as funny if not funnier than what they said. But mostly I went along with this little flirty, silly charade. I seemed to be getting molded into some kind of personality dynamic. The boys said something funny. We all laughed. I said something (I thought equally) funny, they all groaned and eyerolled. It didn't matter. We all had great fun. Sunday afternoons were the best. Often there was one or two carloads of us, all from Monett and then Carol Sue and me, or maybe just me. Sometimes Berta and Di would be with us. But Berta was always with Andy, her boyfriend and short-term husband, and Diana got married right after high school. We drove and drove and drove. We circled the Dairy Queen, went down to the river, or hung out at the park. We laughed and never fought.

On Saturday nights, it was different, of course. There were often dances, at Teen Town in Aurora, or in the park or the Armory in Monett. At Teen Town there were great bands and lots of bumping and grinding on the dancefloor. But you had to go outside to smoke, drink, talk or make out. At the park in Monett there was the park and parking. Parking was the fun of sitting in the front or back seat of a car and exploring the thrills of the body. Kissing, petting, heavy breathing and laughter, running up to the edge, just short of going all the way. You could go to someone's car, make out and steam up the windows. Or you could stroll in the park, swing leisurely on the swings, or do some crazy thing, like strip and jump in the pool, which was dark and closed. You could do something idiotic like climb the water tower, like a particularly crazy friend named Steve did. Steve, like my friend Judy Gay, always had to have booze. If there was no booze, there was no fun. We had to find someone to buy booze for Steve and Judy Gay, or they became depressed, and we, or I, would feel obligated to cheer them up, which was a drag.

But, I thought, somebody had to do it. And even though it never worked, I kept at it.

One night, I went into a liquor store to use the bathroom. When I came out, the person at the register asked if there was anything else that I needed. In about half a second, I thought to myself, "Maybe I could get the booze." So, I said, very casually, like I did it all the time, "Yeah, a six-pack of Bud." And, to my astonishment, the guy retrieved it from the cooler and set it on the counter. I paid him and walked out. No asking for ID, no attitude, just service with a smile. I was a hero that night. Everybody liked me in that moment and for a long time after. I gained confidence and bought booze for all my friends for a good while.

Outside the dance in the park in Monett, our friend Steve climbed the water tower, which got us all worried. The guys became serious and tried to talk him down. He had a stupid grin on his face which told me he wasn't himself. Or maybe he was himself and that was the problem. We were truly afraid he was either going to fall or jump. He did neither that night. But years later, I heard he took his own life, which sadly, didn't surprise me much.

At the Armory, it was a whole 'nother deal. There were long tables around the perimeter of the giant gymnasium. It was dark and people brought their own booze. It was easy to drink there. No one checked ID's and everyone danced, drank and caught the night's primal spirit of excitement and release. The dancing was heady and intoxicating by itself. The freedom in the air was electric. The armory dances were a place of beauty, intrigue and total belonging for me. I was who I was. I didn't care or worry about anything. The night was my element and my escape. My body and soul, dream and reality, love of life and connection to everything were one. I wished the armory dances never had to end.

I was fickle. I liked so many boys that once, while trying to stave off the entreaties of one boy named Freddie, I forgot that I was going steady with someone named Briggsy. His real name wasn't Briggsy, but that's what I called him, because he looked like a Briggsy to me. His real name was David. He didn't mind the nickname I gave him, but I'm sure he would have minded that I forgot we were going steady. In fairness to myself, it was a recent development, and I hadn't exactly put my heart into it at the time. Although I liked him and we had fun together, I never really put my heart into it with Briggsy.

But I did with Sonny. Sonny was tall, lanky, with olive skin and the blackest of hair and eyes. His lips were thin but had a natural red hue.

They curled up when he smiled, like the Cheshire cat in Alice in Wonderland. His eyes pierced and twinkled when he smiled at me. He stood outside the building at Teen Town, where he held court with boys and girls who also liked to smoke and just hang, instead of dancing. I was an insane dancer but naturally had to take a break now and then. To breathe and to smoke and to see who's who and what's what out there. One night on my dance break, I ran into the famous Sonny Buzzard. You laugh, yes, the name was funny. What Sonny stood for was even funnier. But there was nothing funny about my attraction to Sonny, which was shocking and immediate. You could say, he knocked me off my feet. I almost did lose my balance on the slight hill outside of the low, green concrete building on the edge of the park there in Aurora in 1966, the year Sonny was to graduate. There wasn't much said that first night, but it was enough to get us going. Going in the direction of his white 1964 Chevy Impala with red interior for a deeper dive into my breathless dance break. The 1964 Chevy, whose backseat was a turning point in my wild life of sixteen years. And whose taillights would haunt me for years to come.

When Sonny had time for me, we made out. We made out in his back seat, on a blanket in a pasture, with cows nearby, in the front seat, which was smooth and roomy, easy to slide across, fitting nicely under his arm while driving. Talking, laughing, clicking well and sparking wit and quips back and forth. Sonny laughed at my jokes, but could always top them, which never bothered me. We never went anywhere out in the open. We never had dinner or went to a sports event together or walked into a movie at the same time together, though we made out in a couple we bumped into each other at. I was Sonny's sometime girl. Why did this not bother me? It was all tied to my self-image, I guess. I never expected to be Sonny's full-time girl. I took what he gave me. I never asked for more.

When Sonny came to my house once on a Saturday morning, I was sleeping. Mom woke me up and Sonny peeked through the curtains that separated the living room from the bed I was sleeping in, the same bed that was in the bedroom with Mom and Daddy Sag, separated by a rack of clothing. Sonny smiled his curly que smile down on me. I covered my head with the blankets. I never got up, he left. He went to Viet Nam without telling me. Why? Why? Why would he do that? I got a letter about three weeks later. The envelope was red, white and blue. He was a marine, a soldier, a "Lance Corporal." I didn't know how to feel. I loved Sonny, if that was what you called love. I thought about him all the time.

My heart skipped a beat when I saw his car's taillights as they passed by. Who was in there with him? *Was* that him? Where was he going? Were we going together? It was always unclear. There was never loved declared, but always great affection. More than affection. Serious petting, heavy breathing, but I would always stop us right before. Why? Because Sonny wouldn't say he loved me. I required this. I didn't demand it, but I required it.

Once, when he was home on leave, we went farther than we ever had. But Sonny wanted more. I wouldn't allow it. I cried and he gave no comfort. My heart was something like broken. I worried about him in the war, but after ten letters with no reference to love or the unconsummated backseat affair, no inquiries about my life, my heart, my thoughts on anything at all, I got the message. And one night after his return I made an announcement to my fellow female travelers, Berta, Diana and Carol Sue, after seeing his taillights pass by in the night: "I am done with Sonny Buzzard. I never want to see him, talk to him, or ever hear his name mentioned again." This was my first experience of the power of word. Because after this, my heart never hurt when thinking of Sonny. His memory was in some perspective, and I went on with my life, occasionally wondering about him, but never longing for him. It was a relief to reclaim my battered heart, as well as to my friends, who had long tired of hearing empty stories that never really happened. Sonny had been a fantasy, whose occasional materialization served to keep the fantasy going. But now it was over, over for good.

Leaving for Good

When there's light in the soul there is beauty in the person
When there's beauty in the person there is harmony within the home
When there's harmony in the home there is honor in the nation.
When there's honor in the nation there is peace in the world. – Chinese Proverb

When we moved back to Verona from Fayetteville, of course I thought everything would be great. Mom drank more and more. Why? Maybe she was sad. Maybe (as she observed in me years later), she just had "the habit." It was a life she was caught up in. She never confided in me, except to cry whenever I cried, which I hated. "Why are you crying?" she would ask. "Because I want to cry," was often my answer. I had lots of sadness, mainly having to do with feeling lonely, like an outsider. It came and went, and sometimes intensified, like right before my period. Mom was tuned into me, but she always thought everything that bothered me was related to her. Maybe she had the same sadness I had. But I wanted my own sadness. I wanted to feel separate from her, not locked into her and her feelings. We fought sometimes, mostly when she was drinking. She was hard-working, kind and tender most of the time. But with alcohol, the devils came out in her. She and I would go to this and that bar together. Mom drank beer from the can and salted the top. She always got a little salt on her nose, which made her look silly. After a couple of beers, she would ask me to sing with the jukebox. I didn't want to sing. I wanted to sing when I wanted to sing; this was not one of those times. "I don't want to, Mom," I whined. "Sing!" she said through clinched teeth, as though I was refusing to sing to spite her. Finally, I tried to sing a little, but eventually just got up and went outside. She followed me and was very angry. Why couldn't I sing a little for her? Did I think I was too good to do that? I thought I was so smart, well, I wasn't half as smart as I thought I was. On and on it went. My heart felt squeezed, and my mind was a jumble. I loved my mother so much, but at times like these, I felt trapped in a dark box. I needed to break out. I needed air.

We fought so bad one time, I ripped off my own clothes in exasperation, saying, "At least I have my self-respect." Why did I say that? I didn't even know what it meant. Another time I came home from a date. I had a half ponytail with a hairpiece called a "fall" pinned at the top. I got out of the car and my mom met me in the yard, started yelling about something and ripped off the fall. It was hard, loving my mom so much and not being able to help her.

She and Daddy Sag separated again. Mom met someone named Gordon who I thought was a huge step down, even from Sag. But she seemed to like him a lot. The big thing was that they danced. Down at the tavern they danced and danced on that old concrete floor. Mom danced with flair and a big smile. She was clearly happy when dancing. We sometimes played a polka on the jukebox and danced together, she and I. Like me, Mom was always fretting about her weight. She was somewhat round and had gorgeous breasts that she wore high and firm, with sweaters and straight skirts. Or she'd wear jeans and flats with a light-colored shirt that she tucked in. Early on I decided to not tuck anything in *ever*. It wasn't flattering to me, who sadly didn't inherit Mom's voluptuous bosom. I always wondered if that was because Mom asked the doctor to give me birth control pills when I was thirteen, to "regulate my periods."

At night she kept drinking after coming home from the tavern. I pretended to sleep, but that didn't matter to Mom. She would get on a tear about something, something I didn't even understand. Drinking did that for her; it stirred up everything that she usually kept down, like mud when you walked through a creek. She kept raging, kept popping the tops on beer cans. Sometimes there was a lull and I prayed, "Dear God, please let it be over." Then I'd hear her voice or another pop top. It was a nightmare coming from the next room. We lived in Grandma Verla's house now because she had died and it was natural to leave the little house for the bigger, nicer one. I slept in the old dining room. It was open, with no privacy. But I didn't care because I was never there until late at night, sleeping late then dragging myself up for school, if I even went. At seventeen, it occurred to me I could leave, which I did. I left Mom a grown-up note saying this:

Julie G. Olmsted

Mom,

I've gone to live in an apartment in Monett, close to work. It's not unusual for someone to leave home. This is just a little sooner than most. I'm sure it will be better for both of us, and we'll certainly see each other from time to time. I hope it all works out with Gordon. And I'll always love you,

Your daughter

Then Carol helped me move out. Not many boxes, just a few things, clothes and books and stuff for work. I dumped it at the apartment, which was nice enough, and went to work that same day. I was resolved. I felt strong and I knew I was doing the right thing.

An Education of Sorts

I was chronically absent in high school. Boys and work were my thing, and I just couldn't muster the interest. When I did show up, someone would ask, "What are you doing here?" My issue was, I wasn't challenged. I learned this from my husband who learned so much in high school, it still makes me jealous.

Every night, no matter how late I came in, I sat in the middle of my bed and rolled my hair. I didn't need any light. And I could sleep on those huge brush rollers no problem. I had gotten to know my hair and now it was my favorite feature, besides my arms and legs. I was tall, I was only a little fat (but was always on some kind of diet), and my makeup technique was expert. I learned so much at my job at Lakeland, about grooming, makeup, working with others, and excellent service. A few of us would create diets at Lakeland, mostly for three days. Three days only fruit. Three days, no meat. Three days, strictly salads. I learned some discipline and gained some confidence I hadn't had before at Lakeland. Much more than I learned in high school. I was sad there, mostly. I did love choir and writing. But Mrs. Field was the writing teacher, and I just didn't get the chance to stretch in that direction until college.

There was a time I attended school more regularly. It was when I tried out for cheerleader and got it. I was so surprised and happy! I was only the substitute, but I didn't care. I loved it. I went to every game, even though I was the sub. Not every cheer required a specific number of girls. I jumped up and joined in every time they did those cheers. I was enthusiastic and passionate about the basketball team. Once I did the splits in the air and landed on my bottom. It caused a stir, but I kept going. It hurt, but not that bad. This was another example of an injury ignored, minimized and forgotten.

One day the whole team was called to a meeting in the gym. It seemed the rest of the cheerleading team didn't like that I was participating on those cheers. My feelings were hurt, and I began to cry. "I knew she would just start crying," said one of the girls, as she rolled her eyes. I stopped going to games when there wasn't a need for a sub. At least this freed me up to work more.

Later, my back began to bother me. Dr. Hamilton finally put me in the hospital, with traction for my back. After three weeks, I was some better, and was released. I was released, however, to another hospital, a psychiatric ward that gave me the chance to reflect on Sonny, leaving home and my absenteeism at school. I was there for ten days. Mom came to see me toward the end and said, "I want to know watcha gonna do. Just make up your mind. It's up to you." That was like cold water on my face. I thought about her saying that many times. It was true. She was just telling me straight, only I didn't know how to answer. I simply went home back to my apartment and to work. Until I was much older and learned yoga and running, my back gave me trouble off and on for years.

My mentor and confidant in school was Mr. Robb. He taught history and citizenship. I never received above a C+ from him. He gave me no slack, academically. Maybe that's why I trusted him. People talked about Mr. Robb and his relationship with another student whom I didn't know. But Mr. Robb never tried any funny business with me. Even though I regularly came into his classroom, sat in a chair beside his desk, and cried my eyes out. I cried about home, about my friends, how much I worried about what people thought. Once, Mr. Robb sort of lashed out at me: "Would you STOP worrying about what people think???!" He then went into a speech about how it doesn't matter what people think. I sat there stunned. I always thought it totally mattered what people thought. What did mom think? How would Daddy Sag react? Would Daddy be upset? Would I hurt Sissy's feelings? Would Dee like me? The church, my neighbors, friends, just everyone. Maybe that was the darkness I felt so often. Without even knowing it, I was concerned about my actions in light of the opinions of others. Mr. Robb, Mr. Robb. You were such a teacher to me. Years later I called him. He couldn't remember me. And I realized through my tears that he had dementia. My heart broke.

Carol kept driving me to school in Verona from my apartment in Monett, nine miles each way. Then she drove me back to Monett to get ready for work at Lakeland at five. She worried I might not get into college, I stayed home and slept so much. But I had a plan, which was basically to put all my eggs into one basket. Apply to Southwest Missouri State, just a forty-minute drive from my home. Maybe Mom would be more stable then. Carol Sue had the same plan, lucky for me. What would I have done without Carol and her Malibu? I never gave it a thought. I got the idea somewhere that I had a guardian angel. I just assumed this guardian angel would always take care of me. It never occurred to me that Carol was my angel. I had not yet learned to be grateful in my life. You could say I was, as Mom did from time to time, like a "bull in a China closet." Lurching from school to work to boys and bed, then back at it the next day. I didn't stop much and that became a problem that has dogged me most my life.

In high school I never really heard of drugs, just maybe from a distance, like in a movie or the nightly news. But once I had a date with a guy named Harold who had some hashish to smoke. It hurt my lungs to inhale and hold like he told me. After a while reality started to shift. Harold's voice sounded funny, and my own voice sounded strange. Movements of our bodies were a bit jerky and in slow motion, it seemed. We laughed about some silly things. I went to change my clothes and came out in a mint green flowy nightgown. I wouldn't do anything, I just wanted him to see my pretty nightgown. Harold did not understand this and asked me on another night why I did it. When I told him I didn't know, he said I was a prick teaser. I had never heard this expression before, but I didn't ask him what it was. I just felt bad and pulled back from seeing him. It obviously wasn't something he appreciated, being with a prick teaser. Harold liked me, admired me, said I knew where I was going in life. But I didn't know. I didn't know at all. Soon after this conversation, I ended it with Harold.

Something happened a couple of years after being out of high school and going into college. Something happened to everyone, it seemed. I had always loved to talk and dance, laugh and sing. Now, all my friends were most concerned with being cool, which included few of those things. Being cool was the be all, end all, it seemed. We often ended up at someone's house, maybe someone I knew but not always. We sat around with the TV on, sound turned off. We passed joints and never gave a thought to germs or the quality of what was in the joints. I became quieter, afraid to laugh, and very uncomfortable in my solar plexus. I felt reluctant to laugh, also snared into this spell that we all seemed to be under, the spell of having to be cool. Once, I had a talk with myself about all this coolness and where it got me in my life. I ultimately decided I didn't care if I was cool. I wanted to laugh again, be goofy again, romantic again, excited about the day, the sky, the wind, and the road again. I couldn't understand why people liked pot. I did like the effects of hallucinogens, those I took on a handful of occasions. But those trips were rare and for good reason, I knew. The toll they took on my body and the time it took to recover interfered with my work and somehow affected my soul, my whole orientation to the world and if I was honest, my sanity. I kicked this cool thing to the curb. I didn't care anymore what people thought of my disdain for the druggie scene and its weird effects on people's minds and behaviors. Gradually, I backed off from all of it.

But Berta got caught up in all of it. She often had a strange look in her eyes that told me she was seriously unwell. We were driving one night to Tulsa together and got into an argument. I was driving in the rain on the turnpike, driving too fast. The car hydroplaned and I lost control. We crossed the meridian, turning around and around, hitting nothing and no one, miraculously. Finally, the car came to a stop in the middle of the wide field between two directions. Roberta's eyes were closed. Mine were wide open. We weren't high but we were traveling to see a band in Tulsa whose members were high all the time. The line between being high and mental illness was blurred for Berta. She was mad at me but was glad we had the accident because she thought it might kill her. She wanted to be dead, she said. And now she was mad at me because she hadn't died in the accident. The accident, which seemed horrific in the moment, wasn't so bad as it was terrifying. Because the car started, and we continued to Tulsa. After the band got off, we all went to a turnpike plaza about 3am. I thought we were having fun but when Berta and I went into the restroom, she wouldn't come out. She was paranoid. She was afraid of the guys. The fear in her eyes was scary. I worked up my creative juices and outlined a plan for Berta, going along with her paranoia. "If we go with them now, and they start to act weird, I'll say I'm going to get sick, and they'll stop the car. We'll get out then and hitch a ride back to our car. Trust me, it'll work." I was desperate to get her out of that bathroom and for us to get back to Missouri. I would have said anything. But this actually worked. Berta just suddenly snapped out of it. She hopped off the bathroom sink, shook out her long brown hair and smiled. "Okay." When she walked out into the light she simply said, "Sorry, guys."

Doing drugs was like forfeiting all control or sense to the way I related to others, to myself, and to life itself. It made me paranoid, gave me a pain in the gut, and, at times, endangered my life. I wanted nothing, repeat, NOTHING, to do with drugs anymore. Roberta and I became estranged, and she went in and out of psych wards for a few years before she suddenly died in her home. We had some conversation after the Tulsa incident, but it was cordial and without much substance. To her, I was superficial, caught up in the world, not "heavy" enough. It was important now to not only be cool, but be heavy, which meant "deep" and "soulful." I was perfectly happy to be hot and light, whatever all that crap meant.

I did enjoy drinking, however. Drinking was relaxing, sexy, and brought out the fun lover in me. It helped to slow me down, too. Once I was out drinking with friends and came home to a terrible fight between Mom and Daddy Sag. The police were there. The atmosphere was garish and harsh, just like when Mom hit Gary with the cast-iron skillet. Everything was inside out, too bright, too weird. I was pretty drunk, and so all appeared even weirder than usual. I steeled myself and scolded my mom. "Mom, you're drunk." "Why, I'm no more drunk than you are," slurred my poor undignified mother. The officer said, "Ma'am, I know drunk, and this young lady is not drunk." Inside myself, I had to laugh, as the room swirled around me. On the outside I was a cool, collected, concerned daughter, with innocence as my sword and shield. I was a smooth drinker who could hold her liquor well, I decided. Which can be a good thing, and can also be deadly, maybe even more than those other drugs.

Herm

At the end of my freshman year at Southwest Missouri State, I was waiting tables at Lakeland, where I worked all through high school, and was now saving up for the following year. I was able to fund myself through college with loans and grants and the money I made from working. My freshman year had been ecstatic, having had a head-spinning schedule of Philosophy, Writing, English Literature, World Religions and others. I had wept, laughed, shopped and partied through a seismic year of depth, discovery, and a growing confidence in myself and the possibilities that life had in store for me. I was cocky, dreamy, free and happy. After growing up in a small, Southwest Missouri town, drenched with conservative, religious and fearful-of-the world piety, this new world of freedom and academic adventure had intoxicated me. I took on the identity of atheist, feminist, and sexual revolutionist. I made apologies to no one.

Then I took Herman's order in the restaurant. I poured his coffee, set down his eggs, and became a bit weak-kneed. I went back to the kitchen and swooned dramatically to my co-worker Charlotte. "Oh, my god," I moaned in mock fainting desire. "I must have this guy…"

And I did. Somehow, I finagled a date through a mutual friend we called Butter, and there was an immediate chemistry between us that had one thing lead to another. It wasn't long before Herm and I were inseparable. He was nine years my senior, which meant he had an older man attraction for me, while seeming a bit old fashioned and out of touch at the same time. For him, I was a breath of fresh air, a wild bird. Herm was divorced, with a son and a younger sister whom I liked immediately (7 years younger than I was). He was not an educated man, but he was clever and masculine in a countrified kind of way. And he was handsome and rich. At least to me he was rich. His family owned a feed mill in the nearby town of Wheaton. A feed mill and a huge hog farm. It was beautiful in Wheaton, off the main roads, in a valley, with farm after farm visible and breathtaking as far as eye could see. Riding in Herm's 1974 dark green El Camino with a black vinyl top, I learned about soybeans, fescue, corn, hogs and semi-trucks (so many gears, what a turn on it was for him!), all kinds of things even a small- town girl like me never knew. I was so attracted to him he was a drug for me. And speaking of drugs, Herm loved to drink. He taught me to drive and to drink, which I was already pretty good at. We used to have a couple of gimlets before dinner, wine with dinner, then go out dancing and drinking. I was proud of how I could hold my liquor. At this point, it had not occurred to me that I was following a path laid out long ago. My blind spot was my drinking lineage, my genetic history, the convoluted grip that the past had on my future. I had said to more than a couple of dates that I wanted to be a "great lady" someday. How would I make that happen? As you might guess at this point, I had no clue.

The summer nights were flying by. Herm had taken over my life. My freshman year at SMS seemed far away and a bit unreal. I had decided to transfer from there to MU at Columbia with Carol Sue that spring. I was due to begin classes soon and even being away from Herm for a day or so now seemed intolerable. We were attached. We were inseparable. And I had lost something that had just begun to emerge in my freshman year. My independence and my identity.

Herm had a talent for making me believe he was the best thing that ever happened to me. Especially when he drank, he would point out my physical faults and wonder out loud, "Why do I love you? I know that I do, but I don't know why." He made fun of my family, how backward we were. I ate fast and he tried to school me to slow down and recognize when I had had enough. Even though he was country in many ways, his family had money, owned a business and seemed to know the "right kind of people." Then, too, we laughed a lot together. We loved dining out and he often gazed across the table and said things like, "You've never looked more beautiful than you do right now." Herm charmed me, taught me, and messed with my mind. Looking back, I could see he was complicated and a bit abusive.

A Crack Appears

It happened with stealth. It happened right under my nose. It happened like the invasion of mold or peeling paint, like holes in the yard or an invasion of carpenter ants in the woodwork. There was an erosion, a buckling, a breakdown of essential proteins in my psyche. I was entangled, I was in love, and I was developing a mental illness. My confidence sagging, my cockiness crumbling, and my sense of budding discovery and endless possibility becoming overcast and heavy, I one day wrote the following while waiting for Herm to get off work at the mill:

> Lord, where is the sky?
> I see faces, I hear voices
> The clogged valves of my
> now weak senses perceive
> a peace and happiness in the recent
> past, but my God, I can't see the sky~
>
> Where is my calm, my awareness?
> My confidence? (S-h-h, there now, it's
> okay) Mama, I want to
> go home, but there is no home anymore.
>
> No place to run, no place to hide...
> Tell me there is a hell and where it
> Is so I might seek refuge there...
> I feel my feeble knowledge of life and
> beauty locked away in the stupid
> comfort of my childhood. It is gone.
>
> The sky was once so blue, so deep, so
> endless and stirring. I could touch it!
> Now I can't even see it. But I know
> it's there. Is that hope? My body lies cold and
> numb through a cracking mask of fakery. My
> mind begins to scream, "Help me, please!!"

A Crack Appears

Hush, quiet, breathe, look up… (It's not there)

Tomorrow is leering and smiling crookedly,
With decayed teeth and fetid breath. Oh my god,
I want to see the sky.

One hot sunny day we went to the drag races. Herm loved the sights and sounds of a souped-up rig, the smell of gas and oil, the roar of the engines. It was hell to me, although I tried to like it. On this day I was so fragile. I was a stranger to myself. I was nervous, shaky, and fearful. The engines' roar didn't help. I got up to go to the bathroom. On my way back, I lost sight of Herm. I panicked. I cried. I had trouble catching my breath. What was happening to me?

Herman made me an appointment with his family's psychotherapist (seems they all had some time with their therapist, which I'd never come close to). I had so much anxiety I couldn't finish the battery of tests that Dr. Perry gave me. Stumbling into the reception area from the small room I had been directed to for the exam, I muttered, "I can't do this," to the lady through my tears. She took the test from me and asked me to take a seat. Soon Dr. Perry emerged and invited me to his office. I couldn't speak, only sob. He advised that I might have for a time an "island in the storm." It was a few minutes before I realized that what the good doctor was saying was that I should be admitted to the psychiatric ward in the nearby city of Springfield. I needed help sorting things out. I needed safe harbor. I went to Herman's house in Wheaton and packed a bag.

I stayed for ten days. I had a series of medications that alternately helped and caused a serious reaction. One med I took stimulated a severe jerking of my mouth such that I could no longer speak intelligibly. I was on an outing with several other patients at an indoor swimming pool. I told the residential attendant that I needed help. She reassured me that I was fine and that we would be leaving soon to go back to the hospital. I continued to shake and jerk and wait for the others to finish their swim. When we returned, the male nurse who saw me walk through the door rushed to get me a shot. This helped me return to my new normal, a depressed, anxious, confused and fearful girl. Finally, my meds were adjusted properly, and I could function minimally. I emerged from the ten days, not happy and free like I secretly hoped, but sullen, mixed up and still shaking (inwardly and outwardly). I had no idea what the future had in store for me.

A week later, I was planning my wedding. This is what happens when you feel cornered and think you have no options.

Wedding Day with Herm (Can you see the fear?)

I was walking in a bubble. I was swimming in a dream. I was moving in slow motion, with numbness as my overall emo state. I was on medication. "Melarill is used to "treat certain mental/mood disorders (such as schizophrenia)". It "helps you think more clearly, feel less nervous and take part in everyday life." Well, yes. But what it doesn't do is make you happy. What it doesn't do is restore your confidence. And what it doesn't do is help you remember who you are, or were, or thought you might be.

There were some peaceful moments. There were the sounds of summer nights, the bare brown of branches in November, splitting a twilight sky, full of pathos and mystery and beautiful sadness. There were mornings of birds singing and cows mooing and roosters crowing. The most beautiful sounds I ever heard. I hold them inside me still.

You could get married quickly in Miami, Oklahoma. I was barely twenty-one and felt lost without Herman, lost with him, what could I do? We took the hour-plus drive, Herm, me, Mom and an older friend of hers named LL. I wore a white peasant dress with pink flowers and a floppy sunhat. You can see how afraid I was in the one of two Polaroid pictures that were taken. I didn't know how I was supposed to feel, and so, I guess, didn't feel much of anything. What to do on your wedding night? Herm had had surgery recently on his privates to remove some kind of growth. We thought hard a while then decided to go to the drive-in movies. What was showing? A Clockwork Orange.

A Little Happy - Mom, Berta, LL, Herm and Me

In the mornings, Herm would wake up shaking. I felt it before opening my eyes. I would go get him a shot of Jim Beam to "calm his nerves." He never seemed to be drunk. He was just always drunk. I was anxious and miserable and saw no way out. The future was a dark hole. I was working at a bookstore where I nearly fell asleep behind the cash register. Herm went to rehab. He emerged sober, grateful to be alive. Eager to make plans. What to do, what to do? Move to Arkansas, of course.

Why do people always move to Arkansas? I wondered to myself. Land of Opportunity, oh yes. "We'll go to Arkansas," Herm dreamed out loud. "You'll go to the university, and I'll get work somewhere. And we'll have a baby." That got me. "Okay," I whispered. And we started packing.

What did I want to do with my life? Who the hell was I? There were dreams once. Dreams. What was that? Just a word, a stupid word. Something on a greeting card, a poster, a song. I didn't want to dream. I just wanted to look up and see beauty. Hit the open road with nowhere to go. Sing Bye-Bye Miss American Pie. Drink rum from the bottle. Now we're talking babies? Yes, yes. I'm old enough. I love kids. But, what about something I used to want, used to care about, write about? What was that? Who was that? Yes, yes, we'll go to Arkansas, Land of Opportunity. Hills and curves that make you dizzy, drive-ins and shopping centers that litter the land. Biscuits and gravy, grits and fried chicken, Budweiser and Jim Beam. Hell yeah, let's go.

We were headed down there and stayed with Mom the night before. Next morning Mom went to work in the restaurant, and we stopped in for breakfast. My anxiety was through the roof. I smiled as we ordered. Big breakfast. Mom served us. Herm had left his billfold at the house. He left in the truck to go get it. Mom refilled my coffee:

Her: Are you happy?
Me: (looking down, tears falling on my eggs): No. No. No.
Her: You can come home, you know.
Me: (Looking up, whispered) Okay.

Herm walked back into the restaurant. We paid for breakfast and got into the truck.
Him: What's wrong?
Me: I can't. I can't do this. I'm sorry.
Him: Don't say it.
Me: Take me to Mom's.
Him: You bet your ass.

I felt dumped even though I was the one who set things in motion. I had reached the limits of pretense. I surrendered to my despair, my truth, my empty pot. There I was, broken, fragile, no hope, no plan, no view of anything coming or going. From the inside out, I was a dry leaf on a half-dead tree. I sat on Mom's porch and cried and smoked.

We had gone through countless reunions and separations, late night arguments of weeping and gnashing of teeth. How we argued with such precision, intricacy, bitterness and depth! My mother heard us once and commented that we were sick. I was defensive but of course she was right. We were George and Martha, Elizabeth and Richard, Brad and Jen. It could never work, but we kept pretending, that is, until we could no longer. This was the day; it had finally come.

My mother's love and the long, sunny days brought me back to life. I walked the alleys behind Mom's house, feeling the sunshine and thinking maybe I'd be all right. Sometimes I'd get anxious and think Herm was right: *I'd never find anyone else to love me like he did.* I'd put my hand on the phone to call him and draw it back, like from a hot stove. I read, "I'm Okay, You're Okay." I prayed and sang to myself. Once after showering, I put on Mom's terrycloth bathrobe and took a snooze on the couch. I woke up to find her boyfriend Gordon filling me up under the robe. "What are you *doing?*" I asked in disbelief. "You mean I can't get a little bit from you?" He said with a sheepish smile. "Hell, no," I shot back.

I never told Mom about this stupid incident.

I kept seeing a therapist. Dr. Perry recommended that I participate in group therapy. There were six or eight of us and I looked forward to it every Thursday night. I cried to my peers one night that I always feared that people would think I'm corny. A slim shy girl named Patricia said that I *was* a little corny, and that's what she liked about me. I caught a glimpse into who I was again. I thought I was going to make it. Patricia and I went and had a drink together that night. She said she felt like a real human being. I said, me too.

In group therapy I found the relief of being open and vulnerable and safe. Dr. Perry made sure that each person could share openly, without fear of being shut down, interrupted or invalidated. I began to see that I was acceptable, that there wasn't anything wrong with me, that I had worth. I shared in the group I had a near constant feeling of needing permission to speak, of having to speak quickly to get out what I had to say, and a physical feeling of needing to shield my face for fear of being slapped. For years I had the fear of being slapped, wincing at times, a feeling of tensing that goes with the sight of a raised hand. This could be in response to a raised voice, not a hand at all. Of course, as a child I knew nothing of the concept of abuse or even the word "abuse." But in group therapy I saw that I was abused, by my first grade teacher Mrs. Rider and by Big Nola. Inadvertently by my mother, but mostly neglected, overlooked, and sidelined, by a context of carelessness, addiction and domestic violence.

Den

I met Dennis at Sambo's in Springfield. Sambo's. Seems hard to believe now, but there it was, a 24-hour diner that specialized in pancakes. Little Black Sambo was happy on the sign, eager to serve. The lights were bright inside. I had been out with Roberta at the place called "Wine & Spirits." We had had our share. But now it was the wee hours. Now was time for breakfast at Sambo's on Sunshine Street. We were laughing, carefree, not looking for love. Just pancakes and sausage and coffee. But there he was, in the booth behind Berta. Long, full, wavy blond hair. Generous mouth, elegant fingers and a cat-like way of holding his coffee cup. Openly flirtatious. "I'm a virgin," he said once the conversation got going. "Would you say that if it weren't two in the morning?" I asked with amusement. "Probably not," he answered coyly. I liked his smile, his eyes. He wasn't handsome, so much, just incredibly sensual. Something about his hair made me want to grab it.

My heart was fragile. My mind was even more so. I was not yet divorced from Herm. We had been married a whopping two months when my mom told me I could come home. I was so lost, staying back at her house. But grace had brought me home and I felt it, like sunshine, like soup on a cold, bleak day. I walked a lot, just around the neighborhood, her yard, the alley that split the backyards and defined the gardens, just past their full harvest. I felt saved yet precarious, peaceful yet totally unclear. I knew this was a time for repair, for not knowing, for rest and regrouping.

It was hard breaking away from Herman. I continued to look at that phone, wanting to call, longing to call. But calling was what got me into trouble all the times before. So uncertain about the future, my sense of self rocky, patchy, like a painting salvaged from a fire. Only outlines and gauzy fragments of strength, of beauty, of identifying characteristics. But something was coming into view, something was gaining strength, something was healing and reforming, the night I met Dennis at Sambo's. I think he saw it and moved in quickly.

Once Dennis had moved into our booth, next to me, everything else disappeared. His friend Dallas moved next to Berta; they had their conversation, we had ours. I remember Dennis' face filling my vision. I remember his lips and strong, white teeth doing something like melting my insides. I remember paying my own bill, exchanging numbers, him giving me an address.

Time made an appearance again around 5am. I had fallen asleep, but was aroused from blissful slumber by Dennis, readying to go. "Where are you going?" I asked. "Gotta go," he answered, somewhat evasively. "Gotta go where?" I was incredulous. I thought this was going somewhere. It was looking doubtful. Dennis stopped and sighed with some kind of "I've got to tell the truth here," look on his face. "Well, I've got a paper route." A paper route! How old was this guy, I asked myself, then him. "Gotta go," he said again. "I'll call you." Big kiss. Big whopping kiss. My insides smiled big. Oh, it's going somewhere, all right. I got up and got going myself.

I went to Mom's and got into bed. I woke up in the early afternoon. Dennis had called. Mom said, "Who's this Dennis person?" she wanted to know. "Someone I met last night," I answered with a yawn. Someone I like, I thought to myself. More than a little. Something in me had awakened, or healed, or perked up, as mom used to tell me to do quite often. Perked up and lit up. Life was on the upswing.

I was ready for the relationship that taught me I was good; I was acceptable. I was funny, smart, and hot. I was desirable and I had brains. Dennis was not quite as smart or as educated as I was. That was okay with both of us. He used to say things like, "them people over there." I would gently say to him, "those people, Den." "Yeah, them ones." No, the correct way is to say, "those people." The word them belongs at the end of the sentence, at the end of the preposition. "Okay, Ms. Smarty," he would say, "now get over here with them lips of yours." And he'd kiss me, and I would melt. We were in perfect sync.

After I learned he was 17 to my 21, it became no big deal. I attended his high school graduation. I went on trips to the lake with him and his family. They accepted me and treated me kindly. I had bouts of anxiety, but Dennis was someone I could cry with. Crying was a great release and Den had so much compassion for me. I shared my social anxiety with him when I was around his friends. He never said much, just looked at me through big blue eyes of love, then held me close with his sunburned arms covered with soft blond hair.

Den and I did some drugs together. Even though I tried getting high with his friends on marijuana, I still hated it. Why, oh why, would anyone want to do something that made them even more paranoid than they already were? What was so appealing about a knot in the middle of your solar plexus that wouldn't go away? And while we're at it, where was the fun in listening to Pink Floyd's Dark Side of the Moon while watching a stupid TV show with the sound turned off? I was not a fan of this form of entertainment.

But a few times we did mescaline. This (as was my understanding) was an organic form of LSD. These were intense experiences of sensation, connection and deep ponderance of ordinary linguistic and philosophical concepts. When we were alone, the time was truly other worldly. Once I saw the beauty of my face in the mirror, which amazed me. Another time the buds on the trees at night in summer were bright neon purple, and the stars twinkled in the sky with many colors, into the vast infinite deep. These experiences were holy to me, and Dennis always validated my experiences. He thought I was holy, and because of the great expansive space he gave me to be myself, maybe I was.

Of course, we didn't need to be high to be high. Once, while driving in the dark, Maggie May came on the radio. We both knew all the words and sang the entire song at the top of our lungs, like two crazy kids, which we were. Another time we wondered what it might be like to roll down a grassy hill together, then just did it. We lost control as we rolled and laughed so hard it hurt. Several other parts hurt, too, but it was worth it. These were the times of Judy and Dennis. No big responsibilities, no concerns for the future, just day after day, night after night of radical love, ridiculous fun, holy laughter and experiences of deep curiosity and blissful discovery. And, for me, it was a healing.

From the beginning, we knew our time was short. We understood we were not to be together long-term. The amazing thing about him was that he knew I'd have to leave at some point. Why was that? Something was driving me, moving me along, like a shifting wind, that for now, was a gentle breeze. Where was it leading? Didn't quite know, but finishing my college education was as far as I could see for now. I had been renting a small house in Springfield, working at the Holiday Inn in the restaurant there, 6-2 shift. Dennis was with me night after night. He worked at a factory, day hours too. We fell into a little homemaking pattern. We woke early, drank coffee, kissed good-bye and promised to be there at night. I loved it, but at some point in my therapy, I felt the need to move on. Den understood. To this day this perplexes me, the goodness of some hearts. The generosity, the letting go. I was starting to learn to be grateful. I was certainly grateful for him and the strength that was returning to my life, due in no small part to the love he so generously gave me and that I was able to receive.

The last night we held each other and cried practically until dawn. He helped me arrange for a small U-Haul trailer to hitch to my '74 Ford Pinto, which mom had co-signed for, trading in a '70 Maverick I got in the divorce. Dennis packed it to the gills, working alongside me. On the day I left, he planted on me one more long dizzying kiss. He held me close and said, "I will always love you." "Me too, you," I said. How could I leave this? This house, a decent job, an amazing boyfriend who gave me every freedom, except the ones I shouldn't have in the first place. How could I? Slowly, slowly, I backed the car with the trailer out of the driveway and, map in hand, headed toward the big city. I got onto I-71 after getting a coffee to go at the Sambo's. I drove and drank coffee. I cried and kept driving through the rain of my tears.

In later years, after moving to New York and meeting my husband, Dennis gave me a call. He was on his way to the Middle East as a nurse in the Air Force. He thanked me for the difference I made in his life. He said it was because of me, he strove for something higher. Every now I think of him and wish I could catch up, see his face, touch his hands.

Julie G. Olmsted

I Am From

*I am from green hills and blue lakes
Sunrises, cattle, miles of crops and winding roads
Curves can throw you, slow down, see God's
Country*

*Sunrises, cattle, miles of crops and winding roads
Honkytonks, hillbilly twangs, Bud Light and dancing on
Sawdust under the stardust,
crickets, tipsy giggles and sad misunderstandings.
From loving teachers, cornbread and beans, church suppers and
Old-timey hymns.*

*Honkytonks, hillbilly twangs, Bud Light and dancing on sawdust
under the stardust, wandering state to state,
searching for love in nooks and crooks
I'm from hetero, homo, red, blue, country, rock 'n roll,
stories of heartbreak and bounce back, all in a day's work.*

*Wandering state to state, searching for love in nooks and crooks
I'm from tears and fears, stepping out boldly, hiding under a bushel,
From hard work, bad decisions and good gin that makes you crazy.*

*From tears and fears, stepping out boldly, hiding under a bushel,
From outer space, inner wisdom, spaced out and locked in
See me climb the hill, up on the hill, roll down the hill, and
over the hill, sometimes hitting the wall.*

*Outer space, inner wisdom, spaced out and locked in~
From nowhere, everywhere, from heaven above, down here below,
friendships and courage,
I'm from peace and solitude, terror and transformation, Good News
and heartbreak
I'm from joy and confusion, being alive, lost, found, lost again. Here.
I'm from here.*

Kansas City

In my recovery process with Dr. Perry and group therapy, I was introduced to a government program that paid for a big chunk of your college tuition and fees. I had been out of college for at least two semesters, but there was never a doubt that I would return. I didn't know where, but this program was state-sponsored and to take advantage of it, I had to stay in Missouri. Where was it that I had never been? Where could I go, feel I was far enough away from the Ozarks and still in my element? Kansas City, of course. Two things I knew about Kansas City, it was NOT Arkansas, and it was a real city. It was the place of "Kansas City, Here I Come." They got some crazy little women and I'm gonna get me one." I was gonna be one. I didn't have to take a train or a plane. I could just wake up and drive, it turns out. From mom's house in Aurora (where I stayed on the weekends) to my Monday 9am Spanish class it was three hours, give or take.

I continued my habit of waking early to get on the road, loving the drive with little traffic, coffee mug in hand, the sun rising just for me. I carried a small disposable camera and sometimes would pull off the road to take pictures of cows and sunrises. Cows and sunrises, I decided, were my favorite things now. I felt the sun rise in me also. I looked around and saw the sky, deep and blue, not threatening or so big it overwhelmed me. I was young again, too. After a dip into old age, depression and crippling anxiety, something like strength was flooding my bones and my blood. What was it? Hope? A call to adventure? Freedom? I didn't care if I had a boyfriend at all. In fact, it was my committed preference to be unshackled and free to move, to drive, to dance. But first, I had to deal with homesickness.

Homesickness is a real thing. It can feel as bad as a break-up, your heart aching, your mind a muddle, your insides suspended in unsettled space. I knew how to say no. I proved I was able to walk away from familiarity and something like comfort into an uncertain future. I had said good-bye to mom, to Herm, even to my beloved Dennis, with whom I had no quarrel, except the need to move on. The need to expand, to grow, to come into another place of confidence, challenge, peace. But a peace hard-won. Not the peace of inactivity and familiarity. The peace that comes through daring, through struggle, by cracking through the egg of my past and the limits I had innocently inherited. Could all this be found in Kansas City? Could I access it in myself in the context of a city at all? I would find out. I had said good-bye to many things, but never to the cradle of my childhood. Never to the hills and stars, who were my true home, my world, my ground of being.

I found a studio apartment in a decent hilly section close to downtown. I got a waitressing job at a fern bar and restaurant called Strawberry Fields in a mall nearby. I was moving along, but the homesickness was overpowering. Everything was strange, so unfamiliar, unreal. It was summertime and hot. School didn't start for another six weeks. Why did I come early? I had forgotten the logic of getting settled and familiarizing myself with the area. My heart was in the hills.

I called Mom. "Why don't you just come home?" she said. "Because I don't *want* to come home, Mom." This was a familiar exchange. I knew this one but couldn't repeat that past. Mom was just being Mom. I understood that, for her, it just made sense that if I wasn't happy, I should just pack up and go back. But I knew I wasn't unhappy. I was trying to change my damn life. And it wasn't easy. I gave myself three weeks before I'd allow myself to go home for the weekend. I designed a grieving process that went like this: Every morning before getting ready for work for the lunch shift, I'd sit at my little table in front of the window and cry. I didn't have to work at it; I just sat and took a deep breath. I cried and cried for everything I missed: the trees, the lake, the stars, the drive from Springfield to Monett to Aurora, my friends, my mom. Dennis. The Holiday Inn. I missed it all. I cried for it all. Then I'd get up, shower and get ready for work.

One day during my self-imposed, three-week confinement period, I zoomed in on David. David worked as a waiter at the same restaurant as me. (I had never seen waiters, just waitresses. This amused me.) He was in a relationship with Richard, about whom he talked frequently. David was cute and naughty and bitchy. He had brown upswept hair and wore a tiny bit of makeup to hide his facial flaws, of which he had none. He loved to smoke like a 1940's (female) movie star and talk trash, laughing always at his own jokes. David made me laugh, and do the eye roll, which I had perfected. This would make David laugh, which drew us together as friends. I had a friend now, and it took less than three weeks. Two friends, including Richard. I visited them in their house. I watched them fight and make up. And in the evenings, we all would dance.

The Silver Fox was what was known as a gay bar. I had never, of course, been to such a place. But it was natural for me, as mom would say, as falling off a log. It was the height of the disco era, and I grabbed onto it like a lifeboat. How much more fun was this this than sitting in a circle passing a joint with sleepy, haunting music and a muted TV! My body was on fire for dance. Donna Summer reigned. Journey rocked. Funky Town, Love Train, Night Fever. In these I lived and moved and had my being.

Religion was on the caboose of the Love Train at this point. It seemed to come unhinged a bit, so in love with life was I, life with Richard and David and all their fab friends. In three-week's time I had latched onto a new life, even though I would now allow myself to go home to my "straight life" on the weekends. I was no longer afraid that I would leave Kansas City. School would soon be starting, and I was rooted and ready, just like I planned. I didn't know the specifics of course, but now I was glad that I had moved up early. I had known without knowing that getting a jump start would be a good thing. What I didn't know was the culture that I would find myself in and loving. And that I would become what was known as a "fag hag." "Fag hag?" I said with great puzzlement to my friend David. What is *that?* David furrowed his brows and looked at me with that "You don't know, girl?" kind of look. No, I didn't. But I guess I could know if I thought about it a bit. *"A fag hag is a woman who likes spending much of her time with gay men."* Well, yup. That was me. No doubt about it. But I was pretty much like, *so what?* I was having a great time feeling free and making up for at least a couple years of no dancing, and geez, I wasn't hurting anybody. So, what was the prob?

Sometimes Richard and David's fighting would scare me. They would screech and cry and threaten to leave. They never got physical but I always worried that they might. When I was little, my body would tremble uncontrollably when Mom and Daddy Sag fought. If I was in bed with Mom, she would say through clenched teeth, "Stop it. Just STOP IT." I couldn't. This happened a few times at David and Richard's apartment.

Michael

I wanted to move to a bigger place on Campbell Street. In our group was an exquisite boy named Michael. Michael was brilliant, hilarious, and looked like Jesus. His shoulder-length hair was often tossed about through his animated movements and antics. I was drawn to Michael by his humor, his looks and his great mind. In other words, I was attracted to him. How does one manage this kind of attraction? I think by distraction. There were enough of us dancing, drinking, laughing and just entertaining each other, that I didn't really think about it much. It was enough for me to just be near him. And so, it made sense for us to move in together. The rent would be cheaper, the space would be larger, and Michael and I could laugh together endlessly.

The thing about roommates is you don't really know about how they live till you move in. The only other roommate I had had was Carol Sue. She and I were both neat. Carol taught me about grocery shopping, according to the week's menus you had sat and planned out. Every night one of us cooked and the other cleaned the kitchen. The sink was washed out and dried nightly and was just like that when you got up and made coffee the next morning. We had days for laundry, dusting, vacuuming and ordering pizza. These were habits I had learned for life. Michael knocked out these habits like a bulldozer at a construction site. He was the messiest, sloppiest, grossest and most thoughtless person in his approach to home living that I had ever met. He trimmed his own hair and beard and left the bathroom sink full of his clippings. He chained smoked and left ashes and butts in every room. He ate everywhere and didn't bother to clean up and wouldn't have for days, if I didn't tell him to.

Ah, but he was so funny. And when I would get angry, Michael would look at me soulfully, thank me for telling him, and promise to do better. I so wanted to believe him. We continued to laugh and hug and cry from time to time. Michael told me once that I was the most moral person he had ever known. He rolled his eyes as if to say, that he tolerated my sense of morality, even though he appreciated it. I had never thought of myself as moral. Just the opposite, in fact. I was striving constantly to be moral and always failing. It was stressful to strive so much. And I guess that's where dancing came in. I literally couldn't wait to get off work at the restaurant where I had been standing and walking for hours, only to shower off the day's work, put on my best attempt to be an attractive "fag hag," then shoot out to the Silver Fox or any number of other gay bars we frequented. In my heart I knew that was not a bad thing, but there still was this sense of never really being enough, never doing enough, this burden of something like potential or calling. I had no idea what it was, and I certainly wanted to find out someday. Dancing, like driving, helped me forget all this, which was both a good thing and a bad thing.

Once Michael and I had danced the night away, drank a good amount (another thing, Michael drank beer and left empty bottles everywhere), and dropped onto my bed…together. We did something I wondered if anyone had ever done. We kept dancing…with our hands. We held hands, then gently started pulling them apart, then together. We lightly touched and twirled our fingers over and under each one's other hand. It was silent and erotic. It was spontaneous and hypnotic. It was out of time and totally mystical. I told Michael I loved him. He just looked at me deeply and smiled.

The next day I looked around the apartment and sighed heavily. Michael had to move. I had tried everything I could think of to be at peace with his staying. In the harsh reveal of this light, I was clear that day would never come. Not only was there nowhere to go with him romantically, but our living situation was intolerable. I was treading water with Michael. I was not exactly squandering my life but there was no future for me with this brilliant, self-destructive, alcoholic gay man. I gave him thirty days to move out. He pleaded and cajoled. But it was I who was unmovable. And it was he who gave me back my clean, orderly apartment. And my loneliness.

Crossing the Rubicon

I started working at a cool, dark bar at the Plaza Hotel. I was a cocktail waitress, then got the hang of bartending. A brother/sister duo sang after eight, creating an easy, groovy atmosphere. I enjoyed the flow of tending bar, listening to Pam and Peter, cleaning up, washing glasses, making small talk, collecting tips. I enjoyed, too, the attention of the bus boys from the restaurant next door. Especially from one, Masoud. Masoud was impressed with how I pronounced "Iran," just like he did. His friends were friendly, smiling always, laughing at my jokes and seemingly impressed by a female behind the bar. I knew and cared nothing about politics or world affairs. Were you Christian, Muslim, Nothing? It didn't matter to me.

The guys were always bringing in ice for the bar, especially Masoud. He delivered a third time one night, and I laughed. There were four customers in the bar at the time, and I gently pointed that out. Masoud looked sheepish and smiled. Something clicked inside my body. A night soon after that he came home with me. There wasn't any drinking, but we were both intoxicated.

> What are you studying?
> Engineering.
> Where in Iran are you from?
> Tehran.
> What about you?
> Southern Missouri. Small town. Verona. English.
> You are beautiful.
> So are you.
> Your mouth.
> Your eyes.

He picked me up and carried me into the bedroom. He was very strong. I thought about my weight, glad it was down, not up.

A couple weeks later I walked into the bar and had a wave of nausea, some light headedness. I set up a drink and had a fat feeling, not at all bad, kind of plump, satisfied, unfamiliar. A week later I went to a clinic and had a pregnancy test. The nursed called. The test was positive.

On that same phone call I scheduled a termination of my pregnancy.

Crossing the Rubicon

It was a little over six weeks. Shortly before the abortion, Masoud was sitting at the bar at closing time. We were alone and I was cleaning up. I told him something was up. We slipped. He looked puzzled and it was clear to me he didn't understand. I hated to speak the words, but felt I had to. Given my immediate decision, I looked back and realized maybe I shouldn't have told him. I shouldn't have a lot of things. This was a big one. This was crossing a line I hadn't anticipated the consequences of. Masoud cried and pounded the bar. Awkwardly, I tried to console him. "I know you'll be fine," he said. "But what about my *son*?" I had no answer. Masoud left the bar, and the restaurant, too. I never saw him again.

I went to the procedure alone. I thought I knew what I was doing and maybe I did. If I had given birth at this time in my life, what would my life be like? I could hear my girlfriend Berta say to me, "If you're not ready now, you never will be." It didn't matter; I wasn't ready, or so I thought. At the time, I felt certainty. It would not be easy, but it would be okay.

It was later, when it was "the right time" that I began to feel the regret. Later, when the situation was right. Later, when I was in love and could see myself with the father for life. Later, when life did not come so readily, when the seed dropped but wouldn't take hold. Then it did, then it didn't, resulting in the heartbreak of miscarriage.

Later, there was the waiting, trying for months, studying, praying, other things that now seem comical and desperate. I regretted not telling Mom. She was 52. I was 22. She could have helped me, would have, gladly. I regretted not giving it some time, prayer or counseling. Regretted the cavalier way I responded to the gift of life. I was free. I had choice. But it was not a choice without consequence. It was a hasty decision that had delayed but lifelong emotional and unintended after effects. Was it my religion of early life or something even more organic? You can take a girl out of the hills, but…

Walking down the street, running in the park, seeing the face of my boy or girl (now in heaven), the bottom dropping out of my well of being, the weight of my regrets pressed down. Bending over, weeping, sorrowing with no end in sight. Then after church one Sunday at the Interfaith Fellowship in New York City, a woman introduced me to her eighteen year-old daughter. They had met for the first time in the past couple of weeks. The woman had given her daughter up for adoption at birth and her daughter had contacted her when she became of age. It was a reunion of a lifetime, and they were both bursting with the fruit of joy. I was happy for them. I smiled big, feeling weak and gut-punched. *Who could be standing here with me, I thought.*

My husband, two young children and I walked out into the sunshine. As the two of them skipped down the sidewalk, I said I needed to sit down. We stopped at McDonalds, of all places, on West 92nd St. for lunch. As my little boy and girl played blissfully in the "playspace," I took the time to confess. Yes, my husband knew about it. But I had never spoken plainly the words that were weighing me down to the ground. Slowly, punctuated by sobs and long pauses, I told the story. At the end the words came out of my mouth, "I feel like I have murdered." There it lay. This was me. Not everyone, of course. Me. I was not invincible. I was not invisible. I was human, had a conscience, and the way I saw it, I took a human life. Not until I spoke these words was I free from the grip of remorse. Then a bird burst suddenly from the cage of my heart. It could fly now. And I could breathe.

Speeding Up

It was at this point, if not somewhat earlier, that I became a spinning top. I was always busy, busy, but had little direction. I had noticed this tendency before, but it was just fun, certainly manageable. I was my physical self, the rest of me tagged along but got very little attention. What were my emotions? Unclear. What were my plans, hopes, goals and dreams? Equally murky. I was still young, I told myself. My greatest goal, as I had disclosed to a former high school classmate when asked, was to be a "happy person." I no longer was in therapy so that was not a place for reflection and guidance. I had an apartment on the third floor of an old brick building whose key you had to toss down to whoever was coming to visit you so they could enter and climb the three flights to my apartment. I seemed to never stop, from work, to home, to whatever project I thought I'd work on. Like wall-papering the bedroom, which I had never done and no clue how to do. But I did it, scrapping together every last stray piece of navy blue with flowers stick-on paper I could find to cover the room, into the wee hours of the morning.

School began with a delectable smorgasbord of intellectual offerings. I always loved the end of one semester when the next one was approaching, because soon I would select my new schedule. I was most interested in philosophy, psychology, religion and literature. I didn't have any clarity about what I would major in. I had no real direction or professional "pull." My mother never talked to me about it. My professors never pulled me aside and said anything like, "You know, Judy. You would really be a good…fill in the blank. The most I ever got in this regard was a note from a writing professor that said on the top of my last paper, "Keep writing!!!" That was nice, but keep writing what? I didn't give it much thought. Finally, I majored in what everyone majors in when they don't know what it is that they really want. I majored in English literature.

In philosophy class, my mind was blown. I still had my religious roots but didn't pay much attention to them. Until they were being unearthed. When I read Freud, Nietzsche and Simone de Beauvoir, there went crashing every religious idea I had clung to most of my life. My little town church faith had sprung a leak, and I felt I was slipping off deck into the depths. I had to talk to the professor. I knocked and he answered kindly. I cried and told him I was losing my faith. Was there anything he could do to help me? He listened patiently then told me that, while this was an unsettling time in my life, at some point it would all come together for me, and I would be at peace. This sounded unlikely but I appreciated his prediction. I set aside my faith worries, and continued learning about all the big movers and shakers of the world's philosophies. I disagreed a lot, and ferociously, aloud, unapologetically. I didn't know it, but I was being truly educated, something I had long hungered for. And through some kind of process of resistance and acceptance, I was being formed for my future.

Back in Springfield at Southwest Missouri State in summer school, I had met another Carol in a swimming class. Carol and I hit it off even though she was ten years older than I. She was a free spirit and much more knowledgeable about the ways of the world than I was. She had a husband and two children who were living in Brazil. Carol was "exploring" her life and her identity. She rented a place out of town on a farm, made her own yogurt and bread, and smiled so beautifully, with questions in her eyes. Her hair was long and blonde and looked good up or down. She had many flings with many guys, since essentially, she was separated, and her children were staying with their dad while she figured her life out. Carol and I hung out quite a bit then lost touch. Until I moved to Kansas City and we re-connected. Her daughter Kristin was coming back to the states. Where would they land? Where would be good for both of them?

I took initiative and rented the three of us a house. Walking distance to the University and all my classes, also to downtown and the hip section of town called Westport. It was all there. Kansas City was beautiful in spring. I had picked up the practice of running. I continued to rise early and get my run in before everyone woke up. I still smoked, amazingly, but it was beginning to bother me. I got a job in a place called the Souper in the middle of Westport. They sold homemade soups and breads and desserts. Everyone's favorite was the chocolate cheesecake, which was very creamy cheesecake with a thick chocolate icing. My life habits ran in a circle of running, eating, smoking after I ate and then eating to get the taste of smoke out of my mouth. The tension in my body was unbearable whenever I sat still enough. So, I just never sat still. I loved my courses. I loved living with Carol and Kristin. I really loved my life, if I could only manage to slow down a bit. If I could only know how to relax. I honestly did not know how to do that.

Speeding Up

Bite-sized Butterfingers – A Meditation

Close your eyes and imagine yourself sitting in a car, the driver's seat, in a parking lot at night. You have just purchased a pack of cigarettes and a box of Bite-sized Butter fingers. You take a deep breath, open the box of Butter Fingers and begin to pop them into your mouth. You begin to cry. You cry and eat. It is raining outside. You stop crying long enough to taste the candy, finish one, cry a bit, then eat some more. The rain is coming down in torrents. You are cozy and warm in your car. You smell the chocolate. You feel your waist expanding. You breathe some more. You finish the box. There now. All gone. Time for a cigarette. You light up, inhale deeply, start the car, turn on the lights and the wipers and head for home.

Slowing Down

One afternoon, I was sitting in a parked car talking to my totally platonic friend Dave. The sun was shining, and the air was warm. I wanted to be enjoying myself, but I was miserable. I had so much tension in my neck and shoulders, I found myself telling Dave about it. As I spoke the words of my misery to him, the tears began to fall. I cried and cried and couldn't explain why I was crying. I was hurting, to be sure, but I really didn't know this friend Dave all that well and I didn't know what "was wrong" except that even taking a deep breath was painful, so much grief was I holding. Dave had compassion and just sat there with me.

As my sobbing subsided, he said I might want to try meditation. Transcendental Meditation was being talked about by some. I had even heard about it on Marcus Welby, M.D., a show I watched at home once in a while with Mom. I had no hesitation about learning to meditate. They had a TM center near the campus. I took the class and received my mantra. Twenty minutes in the morning, twenty minutes in the afternoon. I was faithful, devoted, never missing a sitting. For two whole weeks I took to heart what the TM guy had taught me. I thought I would go insane.

When I went back for my check-in, once again I started crying. I said to the kind young man, "I've never been so depressed in my life." This was saying a lot. This was natural, my new teacher said to me. You are bringing up for release all your tension, all your grief. "But I can't stand this," my sobby self said. The teacher showed me a way to slow down the torrent of emotion that was flooding my system. A breathing technique he taught me was actually very helpful. How it worked of course I didn't know, but it did help the deluge of tension and grief I had apparently been storing up. I became a dedicated meditator. Once, I stopped in at a restaurant and asked if I might use a closed-off section to do my twenty minutes. I never missed. My tension began to break up as my practice continued. My panic about my future lessened and my running became smoother and less forced. Meditation was working for me.

I began to start stopping smoking, sort of. Again and again, I tried. There was an incongruence about meditation, running and smoking. I was always clearing my throat. I thought I could sing at one point, but smoking interfered with that. I'd be determined to quit one moment, and then I'd get upset by something and grab a smoke. Even if I put those cigs in the trash, I would dig them out at the first sign of a stress event, triggering a craving so powerful, I didn't have the strength to resist. Mentally, too, smoking affected me. I would be sitting and talking to you, but thinking about how I could get out of there and go have a cig. I loved smoking and I hated it. I loved taking a drag in the summer night then blowing the smoke over the little orange coals, so pretty and innocent looking. I was an expert at blowing smoke rings. This went back to Sonny Buzzard, who blew a smoke ring pretty much every time he inhaled, I had perfected the skill. I was one of the guys. I never had to worry what to do next. I just shook a smoke from my pack of Marlboro Lights, Vantage, or Virginia Slims. Outside I appeared to be enjoying every inhale. Inside I was tormented by the notion that this was killing me. I had a smoker's cough and sometimes pain in my legs after a run that always subsided when I had quit for a few days. I understood the quote by Mark Twain: "Quitting smoking is easy. I've done it hundreds of times."

I wish I could say that meditation cured my binge eating. What an appetite I had inherited from my mom and dad! All of us could vacuum up a meal for ten in about ten minutes. That is, my mom, my sister and I. Daddy never ate with us, but when I lived with them for a short while, both he and my stepmom Margie would comment on the huge amounts I could put away. "You eat as much as a forty-year-old man," my skinny and delicate stepmother would say. I, of course, said nothing. What could I say? "You're right, Margie. I'm a pig. Can you help me with my self-destructive snarfing?" Or, "Is that any of your business, stepmother? Here's the thing: I eat as much as I want, whenever I want. It has nothing to do with you or anyone else. So, BUTT OUT." I ate when I couldn't smoke. I smoked when I couldn't eat. The point was, I was run by my passions and my stress. Meditation helped with the latter, but it didn't cure me. I was at least calm enough to carry on, which I did.

Exploring the Vast Unknown

I loved two professors in college. Dr. Rafael Espejo was my first semester Spanish teacher. Dr. Espejo was from Madrid. He was short in stature and grand in being. He yelled his classes. He yelled and grimaced and growled and gesticulated. He swung around on his muletas (crutches) as a triumphant victor over polio as a child. He flashed the lights off and on in the room. He banged on the chalkboard. He called on students spontaneously, as their sleepy, clueless eyes lit up in fear and sudden rapt attention to answer any question he lassoed them with in Spanish. English was allowed only in the last five minutes of class. Class was every blessed morning at 9am, five days a week. On Mondays when I drove up from home, Mom's house in Aurora, I had a thermos of coffee before I arrived at my class. I was pumped. I was tanked and I was cranked. It was thrilling to be with Dr. Espejo, speaking what would become "my beloved Español." I fairly bounced up and down in my chair. I was his star student. I dropped by his office frequently for a Spanish chat. He loved to chat with me in front of colleagues, showing off his prowess as a professor and my mastery as a student.

I made friends. I had lovers. I worked and attended class. I partied and of course, ran, smoked and meditated. There was a war going on inside me, but it was a kind of cold war. I was managing. Kansas City was so beautiful in spring. On my runs I was knocked out by the beauty of trees, flowering bushes and the endless sky. In class I was knocked out by literature. English was my major, not just because I didn't know what else to do, but because I loved it so. I loved the Romantic poets, Wordsworth, Keats, Shelley, Blake. I was amorous of these men. They became my lovers, much like my TV daddies years before. I sometimes felt dizzy after class, one time actually running into a wall. I wept as I read Ode to a Nightingale. I poured over Tintern Abbey, wrote paper after paper and was alternately ecstatic and pensive, dizzy and focused, blown away with life and overcome with longing.

I wanted answers to life's questions that seemed to be posed by everything that I read and wrote about. I had not learned to love the questions themselves, although wonder seemed to be my greatest hobby. I read an article somewhere in a magazine by someone who had taken something called the *est* Training. Est means "it is" in Latin. Two weekends. Transformative. The author of the article had been skeptical. She entered with a detached, journalistic approach. She didn't expect to "get" anything. She was astonished by what she did get. I wanted this. I was going to "get it" no matter what. I called the number and registered. Somehow, I was able to come up with the deposit and tuition fee, $250.00. I had to go to Denver, where I had never been, staying I had no idea where nor with whom.

My roommate Carol did the training before I did. She came back with a somewhat annoying look on her face, like she had a secret and couldn't wait for me to have it, too. I was only a little annoyed, more intrigued, actually, by this look. I felt I had sought this "secret" my whole life and I couldn't wait to grab it for my own. Even on graduation night at my high school in Verona, when Eldon Erwin had asked what I wanted to be in the future I had answered weirdly, "A happy, well-adjusted person, Eldon. That's all I've ever wanted." I think he did an eyeroll. He definitely sighed. Well, here I was, planning a trip by myself in my little cherry-tomato red Pinto. I had driven that car off the showroom floor. It had four miles on it. Mom and I had gone to pay for my 1970 Ford Maverick to be fixed. We were sitting in the showroom outside the service area, and I saw the Pinto. Oh, she was a beauty! Even though there was nothing wrong at all with the Maverick, it paled in comparison to the Pinto. It was unthinkable for me to have a brand-new car. But after speaking to the salesperson about the trade-in value of the Maverick, it just seemed natural. Mom agreed to co-sign and off we went in the shiny new, totally modern "horse." I mused as we flew down the road, Mom could do just about anything once she decided to do it. That was her gift to me. I hold it inside me still.

I was going to break in that pony big-time, with a trip to Denver from Kansas City. The training was two consecutive weekends, with a "completion evening" afterwards, which I would skip, in order to make my trip home and get back to school in time for classes and of course, work. The morning that I was planning to leave, I got up early and went to make my coffee. Something was wrong but it took a few minutes to sink in. I was off kilter. I didn't have my usual zip. I wasn't hungover. I hadn't worked out too much the previous day. I frowned and thought hard. It came to me after a few sips of coffee, which I wasn't enjoying as I always did. I was getting sick. No, I *was* sick. I felt my forehead and decided I was burning up. I called Carol. I had decided not to go. She said to me, "That's totally up to you." I was incredulous. "What do you mean, up to me?" "Up to you," she repeated. "I have no choice here, Carol. I'm sick. What if I get worse? What if I'm on the road and I have to go to the hospital? I know no one, I reasoned. I'm really sick here." Carol said nothing. I could sense she was smiling. What the hell, Carol? You choose, she said, what you're going to do. You're signed up. You made the commitment. You can buy into your sickness, or you can have a breakthrough. Carol was really pissing me off. I hung up. I went back to bed. I tossed and turned a while then threw off the covers. Man, was I angry! I packed my bags, took a cool shower, got dressed and left.

I felt bad but I had air-conditioning, and I was on the road, which always made me feel better. I drove and drove and stretched when I got gas, ate at the roadside plazas along the way and kept on truckin'. I stayed at a Motel 6 outside of Denver and took aspirin to help me get to sleep. My throat was sore, and my head ached. After a fitful night's sleep, I got myself up and headed to the hotel where the training was held. It started at 9am and I was a few minutes late. When I approached all the fresh faces awaiting my arrival with my nametag, everyone looked up and cheered. That was a first in my life right there. Have you ever been cheered for just showing up? That alone might have been worth the price of admission. But turns out I had much, much more in store.

I didn't feel well. We were set up theater-style in a ballroom, where all distractions as far as clocks and artwork were covered or removed. Our watches were collected before we entered the space. Chairs were set up precisely and closely. In front of the room was a stage and two microphones on either side. In the middle of the stage was a tall director's chair with a music stand for the binder from which the trainer conducted the event. On either side of him (there were also "hers" but not this weekend) were white boards with meticulous writing: *the purpose of the est training is to transform your experience of living, so that the situations you have been putting up with or trying to change clear up in the process of life itself.* Whoa, big promise, I thought. I was not feeling so bad, but still had the sore throat. My curiosity and eagerness to "get it" was greater than my physical discomfort, however. I had the usual feeling of smallness, invisibility and insignificance. I was used to that. I settled in for the ride. My first major shift came when the trainer named Randy asked for a volunteer to come up to the chair beside him and "disappear" something. I raised my hand, he called on me and I approached the stage. I wanted to disappear my sore throat. It seemed he did not expect this but took me anyway.

Close your eyes. Picture your sore throat. How big is it? *Really big, the size of a baseball.*

What color is it? *Red.*

How much water could it hold if it could hold water? *A cup, at least.*

Now, how big is it? *About the size of a golf ball.*

What color is it? *Red.*

On we went for a few more minutes.

I came down off the chair and the stage. People "acknowledged" me.

My sore throat, and everything else in my illness, was gone.

This was a process in learning to be present with something. We don't really "be" with anything, the trainer said. We eat the menu in life instead of the meal. It's all "react, react, react." We don't be with our experience. We don't be with each other. We stuff emotions. We don't think, we have thoughts. And they're the same old, same old thoughts, again and again.

It was masterful, this training. Everything they said in certain circles and the movies was true. They called us *turkeys*. They even called us assholes. It sounds awful but it wasn't. The trainers were such extraordinary human beings, with a powerful way of being with us all. There was such respect, insight and wisdom, it was as if the back of the clock of life had been removed and we all got to see how it worked at last. I wouldn't have missed this experience for anything in the world.

Later, when I was volunteering for the organization as I did for the following nine years, I told people that the training consisted of data, processes, and sharing. But in the first weekend of all that, the biggest takeaway for myself and my life was that, at least emotionally and maybe even spiritually, I was quite old, much beyond my 23 years, and, in some cases, I was dead or at least frozen. Slowly, very slowly, I began to thaw out.

Everyone wants to be happy. Theoretically. I had always thought that I wanted to be happy. But I often sabotaged my happiness, only to realize it after the fact. This is what they called "shooting yourself in the foot." I chewed on that saying till I really got it. But, alas, I continued to do just that, although somewhat less so over time. I had always wanted to make others happy. But I often lost myself in the process, not even knowing it was happening. "Are you cold?" someone might ask. "I don't know. Are you?" I might reply. If you were cold, then I got chilly soon. If not, I was fine. This is what I eventually understood as being co-dependent, and I was an unwitting expert. I had learned very early how to smile and be sweet, to stay out of trouble and to get what I wanted, much of the time. Anger was out of the question. Anger might upset someone (like Daddy, invisible but ever present). Sorrow was to be shared selectively, not just when but to whom. I could, some might say, "turn on the waterworks" pretty much anytime. But it wasn't because I was manipulative. It was because (turns out) I was so freaking sad most of the time.

Often, I was what you might call "happy-sad." Beautiful things made me cry. Sunsets, cows, the glassy look of the lake, the sound of night critters and crawlers in the twilight of summer. Stars. Things reminded me of things that I couldn't explain or express. The weight of the world came to me unawares. So many years, so much time, change, death, heartbreak. It wasn't all mine, but I took it. Once my friend's little sister was falling off the steps of their house. I put myself underneath her fall. Why did I do that? No one asked me to soften her meeting with the broken steps below. I wasn't a hero. I just thought it my job to take the fall of my sister, my mother, my friend, the person I just met. It exhausted me and I began to think I had had enough. Everything, it turned out, wasn't my fault after all. I hadn't known that I thought everything was my fault and behaved accordingly. I just realized it in the "process of life itself," as described often by *est* trainers and others. There was some ability to relax that crept into my life. I got more centered and present in my body. More and more I had the sense that the past was truly in the past. I did a lot of forgiving that was like rope being loosened from my torso. It was kind of like the sermon Rusty preached all those years ago. Only it wasn't sin that bound me; it was fear, guilt and resentment. It wasn't confession that freed me; it was seeing and revealing and letting go.

A Personal Myth

She was told at some point to carry the backpack of bricks for at least "several years," for character, for strength, for some mathematical/philosophical fated and faithful assignment. From God? Mother? A stranger with a stern demeanor and an "air of authority?" She couldn't remember now, so many years had passed. But, climbing this mountain, sweat pouring from her brow, envisioning freedom, fantasizing a watering hole in the steep upward incline ahead, wanting a friend, a foothold or better yet, a foot rub from a friend, she summoned what for her was reckless bravery, not the bravery required to climb but the bravery required to buck the past, which, in her opinion, was not all that clear-cut or even true: Why not just let them go? Who would know? Does it matter? So... slipping off the long-held weight, she straightened herself and looked up, feeling strange, cautious but not at all guilty or fearful. She continued climbing as the sun cooled behind a cloud and her thirst abated.

Transformation

I came back to my last year of college transformed. What did that mean? Did it mean I never did anything stupid again? Oh, no. Did it mean that life was easy, and I got the clarity I had sought for my life's direction and purpose? Not right away. What it meant was that I had a context of understanding for my actions and more specifically, my reactions, in my life. I became truthful about my feelings. And, truth was, my feelings were so submerged, I often felt nothing. The interesting part was the more I told the truth about how I felt nothing, the more I began to feel. My happy was happier. My sadness was bathed in curiosity and permission to be sad. (When I used to tell Mom I was sad, she often would say innocently, "No you're not." She later made us all laugh when she would say, "Let's all just be happy, shall we?") I was a mystery to myself, and I stopped hating that self so much. Not totally, but at least I had a little wiggle room. Things that were different included the following:

I kept my word more. I understood I had been blown about most my life by emotions, fears, and circumstances. I realized I was a workaholic. I couldn't stop working, physically working, on any given day. Was this because I had my first job at age ten? Or was I born that way? I continued to meditate and that was lifesaving. When I was meditating, at least I was *doing something*. This served to alleviate my tension and to give me more energy for my life.

I saw my own judgmental nature. I saw that I was agitated, annoyed, bothered and inconvenienced, in my mind at least, by almost everyone. I had impossible standards for myself and others. I became curious about this and tried not to judge myself too harshly for being judgmental. This was tricky.

I saw I was a perfectionist. Perfectionism is exhausting. Rest is anathema to a perfectionist. I always thought I needed to be doing *something*. Guilt pressed down on me when I wasn't busy. (*What could I be doing now? What should I be doing?*) Judgement on myself naturally transferred to judgement of others. Being able to see this gave me space to have some choice in the matter. My judgement often gave in to compassion, then liking, then love. A naturally energetic person can get so caught up in work, they have trouble stopping. This began to loosen up a bit. Not a lot. A bit. Then a bit more...

Transformation

An example of this was a bouncy, honey colored gal named Kimberly. Kimberly worked with me at the Souper in Westport. She had light brown hair with blond streaks, long, with just the right amount of curl. She wore tight sweaters, had a great figure and smiled ALL the blessed time. She was kind of dumb, kind of funny, very, *very* cute. She annoyed the crap out of me. There was a moment, as I was judging Kimberly harshly and intently, when some light emerged in my head about my attitude toward her. *Why are you doing this? What is it that makes you so harsh with her?* I didn't like my answer. Of course it was that I envied her. I envied her looks, her figure, but mainly her lightness. In that moment, I lightened up a bit myself. I drew closer to her and cracked a joke. Unbelievable as it may seem, we became buddies. It's happened so many times now, so many times. This was a direct result of doing the *est* Training. It has been one of the best gifts of my life.

My persistent longing landed gradually upon the distracted and delightful charms of another mentor, the other professor I loved. Dr. William McKinley was my professor of classic playwrights. His ability to make the plays of Chekov and Ibsen dance in my heart like personal magicians was disturbing. I wanted to psychically dine on these plays. I wanted expository lecturing, in-depth discussion, connecting the dots of ennui with luxury, privilege with decay, despair with courage. All this combined with the stature, warmth, and blond, Irish beauty of the professor was almost too much for my mind and body to contain. I exploded inwardly intellectually and occasionally outwardly physically in passionate alone time with these geniuses of humanity and life of the mind.

Days went by in class with Professor McKinley. I watched his every gesture with liquid dreaminess. Dreams of him continued long after class. I saw his face while running, writing papers, had visions of traveling to exotic birthplaces of the playwrights we studied, hand-in-hand, sunning ourselves and diving into waters of blue, oceanic desire. I had to tell him. No matter the outcome, regardless of circumstance, his or mine, he had to know of my love. But how would I do it? Sorry to say, not very creatively. I made an appointment to see him during office hours. I approached his enormous desk, that stretched for miles. I was small and awkward. He was Adonis at the top of a mountain of papers and handsome gadgets, gifts from adoring female students, no doubt. I sat, unrehearsed and clumsy.

"What can I help you with today?" a natural question. I said something about the difference between Ibsen and Chekov. I liked Ibsen but found him annoying next to Chekov. Ibsen seemed to bludgeon you with his point. Chekov was subtle and let his characters tell you the point, which wasn't always clear but indicated in such a way that you entered the life of the characters and found surprises and gifts that were sometimes embarrassingly like your own life, blah, blah, blah. You know what I think about this? And about that. And mumble, mumble, you know. The professor looked confused but polite and a bit antsy. "And, do you know…that I love you?"

There it lay. On top of the desk, amid all the papers, like a silly paperweight from a tacky tourist souvenir store. I was mortified. My face lit up in fire. My limbs like Gumby. I wanted to jump and run but how could I after such an awkward revelation? I sat, dumb, limp yet leaden. He did the best he could to answer. I have a wife, I'm in the middle of a divorce after a painful affair. I couldn't possibly pursue, anything like a "dalliance," and so on and so forth it went. I managed to stand. I said something puny and polite like, "Thank you for your time." I walked quickly to the door and out into the garish sunlight. It was over. I had spilled my guts. That was me, and I hated myself. But somehow, over the ensuing days, I completed the semester with some shreds of dignity and managed to shake off the humiliation that comes with the vulnerability of intense self-disclosure.

———

I wish I could say I was more directed. I wish I could say I became a famous writer or actress. I just trudged along, moving in the direction of becoming that "happy, well-adjusted person." I graduated from UMKC. I invited Herman and his son Chris to the ceremony. I invited my mom and sister, my Uncle Bob and my dad. Everyone came but Daddy. He never had the money, the time, the whatever it took to do much of anything besides watch TV and work in his auto-body shop. I gained insight into why it didn't work out between him and my mom who, in her world at least, could do anything. I forgave him. I had compassion for his self-imposed limitations. I forgave my mom, and we became closer than ever. I almost forgave myself for my stumbling and distracted longings and efforts in my life. Almost, but not quite.

Starry Sky

One night while sleeping, the starry sky woke me up. Even though we lived close to campus and the Westport area of cool restaurants and clubs, the stars were visible, bright and close around the house we were renting that last year. There were steps leading to a side door we seldom used (Carol, her daughter Kristen and I) and as I threw on something for protection from the possible night chill, I headed for those steps. I didn't know what I was doing; I just followed the prompts of the spirit that opened my eyes and nudged me outdoors. *There I sat looking up, looking up, looking up. The stars, like the sea, I thought, held one's attention endlessly, though there's seldom new patterns or movement or out of ordinary fragments of things to behold. Still, there's endless looking that somehow fills a hole inside of me, I thought. It fills me in. Gives me drink. Fills me up. Fills my cup. It flows in and out. I'm all but disappearing, I thought. Into the night I go. I go. I go. And then, the tears came.*

The tears of years, it seemed. Gladness, joy, pain and longing, beauty and sadness, all of it. All of it. All of it. I was gone now, and no one was there, but the fullness of life, the shining into darkness, the undulating waves of lives and centuries and tiny moments, ancestors and mountains, planets and galaxies, mother and father and child. I hugged my knees and rocked. So much love was washing over me, and I could not stop returning that love. I love you, I love you, I love you, I whispered again and again. I was held in the most beautiful light I had never imagined before. Then stillness overtook us. The world and I, hanging in space, quiet and glowing, peaceful and undisturbed. I lifted my head once again, smiled up at the night that held me and loved me, and went back to bed, to some kind of blissful slumber.

Cornbread in Heaven

Coming in from the cold air, the aroma of a love-cooked meal of meager means filled me with the thrill of peace and hunger: hunger not just for food, but hunger for home, for mother, for comfort and rest. I was ravenous and I didn't care who saw it! I walked closer to the smells and then I saw her. I grabbed my dear mother and drew her to me. It had been so long, a lifetime, really. When my mother had died on May 5, 2004 I was worried I might never see her again. But here, in heaven at last, my worries all faded like a dream of earth, a dream of the past the details of which I no longer could quite fill in.

"Mom. Mommy. Mama. Mother. My whole life I had experimented with the sounds of one and the other. Now they rolled into each other, rolled up sort of, like a juicy fig ball rolled in coconut, with a surprise pure chocolate center. "MMMMMMmmmmm..." was all I could get out. I breathed in her famous fragrance: White Shoulders, oh from the gods, from heaven itself, she used to say, and turns out she was right. Her precious hair, all wavy and shiny and dark, not a strand of gray, her face luminous, no glasses, her eyes bright and filled with that zany combination of mischief and joy, dark and darting, happy and filled with secrets to impart at just the right moment. My dear mother and me, here in heaven. What a joyous, radiant, glorious outcome of the silly dream of dying.

"Mom, are you cooking?" I finally was able to get out of my throat. "Yay-us, can you believe it?" They told me I could do whatever I wanted in anticipation of your arrival, and this is what I chose." "Is it brown beans and cornbread?" I whispered with a mix of emotions I could not define or separate out. "Of course, Sugarbaby! What else would I fix for my darlin' daughter on the day of her homecoming?" It smelled heavenly... A table was set for four and I asked her about the empty place settings. "Oh, you can't guess?" she said with that familiar cat and mouse game in her tone. "Well, yes, I can but I'm not sure I want to." "Now, what do you mean by that?" Knowing full well what I meant but playing innocent, as always. "Well, whoever it is, I'm okay with it, because, after all, we're in heaven, so it can't be bad." "This is true," replied my beautiful mother, setting down large colorful bowls, napkins and glasses. I grabbed the lightest silverware I had ever touched, radiant and new, placed a knife, spoon and fork around each place. Candles in the middle of the table lit themselves, as if on cue from the silverware. Country music began to play softly..."Today I started Loving You Again." Tears sprang to my eyes as I heard *the Merle Haggard song we used to sing when I was a child. Mom set chopped sweet onion on the table (maybe the source of tears?). The music grew a bit louder and someone began to take shape in the distance: a slim young woman, beautiful smile, twinkling eyes of love and joy. It couldn't be. There's absolutely no way. This was no exhausted, obese and disgruntled, limping and complaining, self-absorbed sibling, who pestered and smothered and leaned on me till I wanted to scream. This was my beautiful happy sister, the one I suspected was under the weight of all that fat, all that heartbreak, all that comparing and despairing that I was the beneficiary of, in our lives on earth.*

My sister's complaints about life, about me, about how unfair everything was weighed heavily on my heart and shoulders all my life on earth. She compared us constantly and without a sliver of perspective. Where was her life in all this? She went underground in the effort to justify her existence up against mine. It was a tragedy of generational proportions. But now, look at her. Youthful. Radiant. Slim. Whole. So, this is heaven, this is what we alternately feared, sang and dreamed about. And now, it's here. God is indeed great.

Mom began to dish out the beans. Fragrant. Steaming. Filling the senses with joy and comfort and home. My sister hugged me with just the right intensity, just the right timing. So many times on earth she would ignore me when I walked in the door or hug me so tight I could barely breathe. I always wondered, is she really glad to see me, or does she want to kill me? These were not easy feelings to have. But, here in heaven, all that had disappeared like mist or a movie I was glad to have be over.

We sat down. "One more surprise," said my beautiful young mother, or rather, almost sang. I had just started to mash my beans a bit with the fork, sprinkle on some onion and crumble a huge piece of cornbread onto the creation, when I looked up and there was the last person on earth I expected to see, standing at the open place setting, pulling out a chair. My dad was a sight for sore eyes. Coal black hair and lots of it. His big muscular arms bulging out of his brown and white striped pullover shirt, the dark hair on his chest peeking out of the two-buttoned V-neck collar (his "more-hair sweater" he called it on earth). Daddy smiled and said, "This smells really, really good." I don't remember him saying things like that. That's what my husband used to say. (And where was he?) But, of course, I wasn't old enough to mark those kinds of things when he left us. Daddy seemed normal, like he was expecting us all, like he had been here for a good while. He winked at me and tears started falling like stars from my eyes. He opened his arms and I walked over to him.

Julie G. Olmsted

I sat easily on his lap. I felt his strength as he closed his arms around me. I allowed my head to rest on his shoulder, tears just falling and falling, but he didn't seem to mind. "I'm sorry, Sugar." he said. "I'm sorry for everything." "But, we're in heaven," I blurted out, half crying and laughing, too. "We're in heaven and there are no tears in heaven," I said, remembering the hymn we sang at my grandpa's funeral. "They're not real tears," said Daddy. They are just earth residuals. And see how shiny they are? They're like crystals. And they bless those left on earth." Wow, I thought. My tears are blessings to those on earth. And what about all those tears I cried back then? I was thinking. Those tears were blessings, too, said my mother. Only she didn't say the words. She thought them. Or, rather, she sent them, into my mind. I looked up and she smiled with benevolence. My beautiful mother. My strong, handsome devilish dad. Here, with my sister and me, like I never had it before back on earth. Like I always prayed about at night in my little bed. I looked around the table and we were all smiling and looking deeply at one another, like we never dared to in our lives on earth. Then we took a long breath of gratitude and the smell of beans and cornbread filled us with happy anticipation. "Let's eat, y'all," said my handsome daddy. And we did.

Aside from my classes, my running and the quasi-management of my weight, my carb and nicotine addiction, there was my work life at the Souper Place to Eat in the very cool section of Kansas City called Westport and my immersion in the Backstage Workshop. My friend Joe had told me about this place. Jerry and Lillian Funk, owners and proprietors, taught acting and singing classes, respectively. They were, I'd say, mid-forties, pleasant, fiercely dedicated and intelligent, and ran the small school with good humor and great encouragement to all who matriculated there. It was a grooming school. Everyone, at some point, was expected to fly off the wire and land in New York City. That was the game plan at Backstage Workshop. I was intrigued and in short order, fully on boarded with this plan.

Jerry sat hunched over a desk in the corner of a dark room with ascending theatrical seating for students behind him. In front of us was the stage, a large space with room to experiment and move freely. Jerry smoked Vantage cigarettes, one after another, filling a huge ashtray by evening's end. We studied the Stanislavsky method, which was all about character immersion and back story that was created by the person inhabiting the character, giving him or her the motivation to act and speak in the ways they did. "Behaving authentically under imaginary circumstances." There was an acting partner and there was a "task" in every exercise. Dialogue was narrow and focused on the task and the relationship. There was repetition and response to given reactions and expressed emotions. It was exhilarating and deeply satisfying, akin to sexual activity or a lavish feast for two by candlelight and soft music. Wine, violins, flaming desserts. All of it, only a bare stage for two and loving onlookers.

We all were close. We hugged and kissed without reservation. It was genuine affection with no strings, no expectations. Just unabashed support for the big trip to New York. I was there for almost two years. Joe and I planned our trip to the Big Apple.

Then we went to California. It was a road trip to end all road trips. Who ever heard of moving to New York via L.A.? That's nuts. But that was the plan. Joe was tall, amazingly handsome and of mixed race. That never even occurred to me, but also it never occurred to me to consider Joe a romantic interest. It just didn't feel that way. He was my brother, my confidante, my pal and my acting partner. Joe was interested in the New Age. He read the Bible, the Bhagavad Gita and other sacred texts. He was big on "creating with God." He was, at times, too positive and transcendent for me. I got down and melancholic at times. I wasn't ready to say I had created everything. I still had that old-time religion rattling around in my soul. I appreciated him madly, but sometimes Joe's take on things seemed too way out.

It was an easy quality to forgive, however, because Joe and I laughed and talked about other things, as well as the ones that made me a little squeamish. Our big thing was dancing, however. Joe was a larger-than-life dancer and when we cut a rug, he made me larger-than-life, too. On the way to LA we saw a flyer about a dance contest in a big loft somewhere in Colorado. I bought a scarf and tied it around my head as a turban. I donned a caftan that I had brought from a middle eastern store in Kansas City. Joe wore all white with thick-soled 70's boogie shoes. We wowed 'em. We won the contest.

We got to Southern California all in one piece, except for the time I swiped the car against a railing while Joe was sleeping in the back seat. How we made it in that maroon '64 Chevy is a marvel. It just kept going and going. Then we were there.

In *est* they called volunteering "assisting." I was enthusiastic about this work, this "technology," as they often called it. I had spent a year of my life without any exposure or connection with it, except my roommate Carol. We relished in our transformation. We were so into "being" and being with each other, I sometimes wondered if we were in love. Once we sat talking at the kitchen table having coffee. We were enjoying each other's company and suddenly we looked so deeply into each other's eyes, it was uncomfortable but fascinating. We startled ourselves and laughed our way out of the moment. But, we both had too many boyfriends to investigate our sexuality with each other. We were just soul sisters.

Carol had moved out there to Newport Beach. Joe and I stayed with her for a while. My first assisting job was receptionist on Thursdays, 10-2. I often called in to say I would be late, I couldn't make it, or some other BS. The Center Manager Barry wasn't having it. I had little accountability in those days. It might be raining. Couldn't make it. Bad hair day. Sorry, won't be in. Car wouldn't start. See you next time. But eventually it sunk in. I showed up when I said I would. My word mattered. Mine. I mattered. Showing up and answering the phone, yes, that mattered. We played a ridiculous game that I resisted but eventually got into. It was called, "create a call-in." That meant sit there and "create" someone calling in to register for the *est* training. You might think being a receptionist might involve doodling on a notepad, filing your nails, or making a list of private and personal goals. No. You had to CREATE. My friend Joe was all about creating your life and your future. I was all about, oh, I don't know, enjoying the birds, looking at the sky, planning my outfit for the day, stuff like that. It was that little receptionist volunteer job for twelve weeks, where I learned the power of intention, the importance of Word, and the possibility of creating. On my last day I started to express my thanks for this learning and the words caught in my throat. For the first time in my life, I cried tears of gratitude.

I continued to assist, eventually enrolling in a leadership program designed to train you to lead seminars for guests. It was a roller-coaster ride of agony and ecstasy. That experience I had with Carol back in Kansas City, the one where we locked eyes and felt a powerful connection? I felt with countless people. The honesty, the sharing, the sheer joy of service and knowing that something you did made a difference in someone's life, was, I felt, something I had longed for, been designed and destined for, my entire life. I walked, talked, ate and slept this transformation. I had a love for the creator of the training Werner Erhard that bordered on adoration. Once while running alone in Irvine, California, among the eucalyptus trees, I had a bout of sorrow that he would die someday. I put my arms around a tree and wept.

I met Werner one time only. It was at a fancy brunch in New York City, in honor of those who assisted. The atmosphere was joyous, electric, warm and radiant, like heaven, is all I can say. The tables were exquisitely decorated, with small Christmas ornaments and glittery confetti, tastefully scattered. My heart was at peace, and I had not one iota of social anxiety. I had the profound sense that I truly belonged. At one point I stood behind someone waiting to get a hug from my teacher, and in a way, I guess, my guru. As he was completing his hugging of the person in front of me, he reached out for my hand, sensing my shyness. Then the person was gone, and Werner looked at me in that same way, deeply, with love, with knowing and high regard. He pulled me into his embrace and the thought sprang into my mind, "My God, he knows me." And I know him. Where have we met? I briefly thought. Then I understood. He knows me because there's only one of us here. This moment of awakening, this startling truth, this breaking out of myself and my past, will stay with me always.

I assisted nearly every day. In the office where we checked in, worked the phones, made copies and had meetings, we wrote down in a large book our names, when we started and when we left. Once I counted the hours I had been there in the past week: sixty. During the day I worked lunches at a cheery restaurant. Why didn't I have a job pertaining to my freshly earned degree of B.A. in English? Good question. No answer, except that waiting tables gets into your bones and it's easy money. Plus, my real "career" was transformation. I couldn't get enough and three times I made a plan to "go on staff," that is, make it official that this was going to be my life and my calling. Something held me back and I hesitate to even try naming what it was, but I think it had something to do with freedom, something to do with a different path I wasn't aware of yet.

Vegas

Out of the blue one day, I got a call from Uncle Bob. Uncle Bob was Daddy's brother and we had always clicked. He was handsome and outgoing and had his own band and club in Oklahoma City. He was retired career Army, confident, funny and fastidious in dress. He was traveling to Vegas and wanted to know if I would like to fly out and meet him for a night on the town. This was such a thrill for my excited, trusting, transformed heart. He made the arrangements and I eagerly followed through. We laughed, drank, talked and reminisced about my dad, their mother and other things. I was treated like a princess and decided I could get used to this kind of royal treatment. After sleeping on couches, airbeds and pallets on the floor for the past several months, it was a big shift for me to enjoy this exotic buffet of delights.

Uncle Bob and Me in OKC

After dinner we wandered around the casino. I tried my hand at one bout of blackjack. I got so excited at the prospect of winning, I decided that this was not for me. I liked being excited all right, but not about winning a few dollars, even winning a few hundred dollars. What if I lost next time? How would that feel? I determined that I would not be a gambler. I had enough to deal with without that flashing sharp knife in my hand.

In the Training we had learned about two games. The game of win/lose and the game of aliveness. Win/lose was a cutthroat game, its motivations clear and fraught with danger. Incredibly, that's why we like it. We go to Las Vegas, said my *est* trainer, not because we can win, but because we can lose. The prospect of losing is as attractive as sex, even better sometimes. I decided I didn't want to play that win/lose game. I guess I knew myself too well to get involved in it.

But not too well not to get involved with Uncle Bob. His charms were too much for me. I honestly think both of us thought this "going to bed together" thing was not wrong. It was the seventies. We were both adults. Yes, he had some twenty years on me. But there was something about Vegas that made this little affair seem harmless, right, even. ["What happens in Vegas stays in Vegas."] But it wasn't. It wasn't, because the sweetness that flowed between my uncle and myself developed a bitter component after that. Not altogether, but never the same. It was once and once only. But that was enough to plant a mushroom of regret that remained until I could no longer tell him I loved him. I could no longer talk it out, get perspective, or even acknowledge our mistake. It's not good to do these things. It's questionable whether to tell them. But I have some understanding of this dream-like evening that I can let go of with bittersweet good-bye.

I auditioned for a band in Las Vegas called Ward Burton and Friends. I didn't expect to get hired, but I did. I wasn't a great singer but a good performer with a good ear and some good notes. In my heart and mind, I was in a place of innocence and purpose in California. I loved life and I loved what I was doing. It's curious what the lure of flashy lights and a stage can do to a person, no matter how settled or grounded they are. I don't know if I was settled but I was grounded in my love of what I was doing, but I gave it up, POOF!! Like that.

Letting go of things is one thing; throwing things away is another. I threw away the life I had in *est*. I walked away and into a way of life in which I had no expertise or experience. I was part of a band now. They had their concerns and interests, none of which faintly harmonized or complemented mine. In a short time, I was miserable singing behind the bar at the Plaza Hotel Bar and Casino. I took pictures and sold them on the spot to customers three nights a week at the Sands and MGM Grand.

I had expert people training in *est* but that was something I knew would transform people's lives. Pictures were great but they couldn't come close to the gift of life the training offered.

So, again. I quit. I walked away and you know where I went? Oklahoma City. Uncle Bob had asked me to be a part of his band. It was exciting but a bit scary. I was supposed to be going to New York. I had spent time in California, Las Vegas, and now…Oklahoma? If I had thought about it, I would have realized going to Oklahoma City was almost like going to Arkansas, and Arkansas had never worked out for me. I needed a caring parent to guide me and tell me I was headed toward a brick wall. But that was not available. Daddy was happy to have me coming back to his neck of the woods. Mom was just a state away; she sure wouldn't complain. So, off to OKC I went, with my hazy dreams of I don't know what. This was a lost person with something good to offer the world. But that something wasn't on a smoky stage with a bunch of cowboys sitting around drinking whiskey and Coors beer. But I didn't know that. So, I went.

Oklahoma City

Al Simmons was the sax player in the band. He wasn't particularly handsome, but he was cool looking, with glasses, a beard, and a beatnik way of walking slowly, like to a beat in his head. And he looked at me like someone who had taken the *est* training and assisted a couple of years. Amazing. He liked me; he courted me. He charmed me. Then he told me he was married. Married! What kind of course was I on in my life? I resisted Al's attentions with a vengeance. No, I don't want to go get a drink. I'll get a drink but that's it. I'll see you but no funny business. I'm not going to see you again. This is it. Good-bye. Repeat. Again and again. I was angry at his excuses for not leaving his wife. I was miserable at not being able to walk together and share our love with the world. And I was so lonely on those many days when he had to be with his family, leaving me to wander the bare apartment I had hastily rented and could never call home. All this, followed by laughter, plans to divorce, run off, get married, blah, blah, blah. I hated myself and I began to hate the band, hate Al, hate Oklahoma, hate myself. How did I get into this morass of deception and aimlessness?

I called the *est* office in Dallas. Yes, of course they had a seminar I could enroll in!! They were so happy to have me, welcome home Julie!! Only, my name wasn't Julie yet. It was Judy. Judy Green. I didn't like it, but I felt I was stuck with it, at least for now. I managed to pay my tuition for the seminar: $50. They put me in touch with someone who drove the three hours each way from Oklahoma City to Dallas every Tuesday night. We shared the driving and gabbed about our lives and insights. I was "back home" to a place I'd never been. The lights were turned back on in my life. In my seminar I understood why I had been so miserable, why it could never work with Al or with Uncle Bob and the band.

Julie G. Olmsted

Beatnik Al and the band in OKC

My integrity was in pieces everywhere. In my seminar I started to put things back together. I made a plan to move to Dallas. New York had to wait. One rainy night Al took me home to my dad's where I plotted my move. We were sitting in his van, and I had the familiar feeling of being small, shaky and invisible. "Baby, please don't go." Hmm, I thought. Nice title for a song. "I'm going, Al."

"Just give it some more time. Soon I'll be able to break free and we'll make a life together." I felt myself weaken a little. "I'm going, Al." Deep breath. I'm going and I don't want to see you or hear from you ever again. Don't call. Don't come. Don't write. I mean it. This is it." Something stirred inside. It was familiar but tiny, a campfire in the deep woods. Good-bye, I said. I pulled my red raincoat close, raised my hood, and got out of the van. I walked into my dad's dark house and slipped into bed in the guest room crowded with furniture and junk from flea markets. I slept fitfully then got up the next morning and moved to Dallas.

Dallas

Dallas was big and friendly and welcoming. I house-sat a nice apartment while a new friend from my seminar went away on business. Art was straightforward, generous and busy, always very busy. He was to be gone for three weeks. I got a waitressing job at a converted tortilla factory called the Dixie House. I felt at home there and enjoyed being with my co-workers. One cook in particular, I enjoyed a lot. He was a Mexican "mojado" (wetback) named Armando. Dark and classically handsome, with thick straight black hair and a handlebar mustache, Armando was disarmingly charming. I loved speaking Spanish with him and making him laugh. We ended up hot and heavy until one day an older woman named Maria who also worked there told me the scalding truth: *Armando was married*. I felt blindsided, confused, re-traumatized and deeply angry. I resisted Armando's advances ferociously once more until one day I was free. It helped to get fired from my job. I came to work one day and was told that I had messed up on the schedule. I didn't come in when I was supposed to. Unable to reach me. Sorry. So long. Good-bye. And good-bye to Armando. Dodged a bullet there, but still had burns on my heart. I was, in my mind, a for sure loser in love.

I threw myself into assisting. I spent so many hours on this or that team, as team leader, on phone banks, in guest events large and small. I sometimes referred to myself as a "new-age nun." There were moments of such joy, such calm and such satisfaction, I really did believe at some level, I had found my true calling in life. Once, at a large-scale guest event in a very elegant hotel, I was spinning around, being what was called "on purpose" in my every move. I turned and looked up as the seminar for guests was about to begin. I stopped with a jerk when at the top of the escalator I saw him standing, watching, smiling. It was Al. I didn't know whether to turn my back and head into the large room or walk up and say hello. I did the latter. "Hi, baby. I told you I'd do it. I got divorced. I'm hoping you'll take me back." The words sort of flowed together like muzak or CB chatter. I noticed I felt nothing. I said, "Sorry. Can't help you. That's over. Gotta go." I walked away feeling a strange mix of strength, sadness, curiosity and victory. I wondered if I was meant to always be alone. I had the thought I might be okay with that. I took my place among my team. I was on purpose.

I bounced around some more in Dallas. I worked as a secretary for a trucking company. I showed apartments for a fancy complex. I continued assisting, loving what I was doing yet feeling a growing sense of discomfort with my living situation (unsettled) and future (hazy). It was the year John Lennon was shot. It was three years since I graduated from college (those happy golden years). Those of us who assisted regularly often went to restaurants, to hang, to chat and chew and *be*. It was after an evening in a home guest event a friend of mine led, that we went to a nearby late-night café. We ordered our food and he turned to me. Someone had showed up at the guest event and left early. This someone was my guest and someone I was seeing casually. I didn't expect him to leave and had gone to the kitchen to speak with him privately, urging him to stay. He didn't. The leader Ron was someone I looked up to greatly. I appreciated his rapt attention, his support of me as a person. He looked seriously into my eyes and said, "That guy tonight? The one who was your guest?" Yes, I said. "You're seeing him, right?" Yes, I said. "He doesn't represent you. You need to stop fooling around with these guys. These guys are doing you no favors." Oh. Oh. Oh. I was embarrassed and exposed. I was sobered and roundly upbraided. This guy looking at me, talking to me straight, was speaking the truth in love. He had no reason to say this other than unconditional support. He was happily married. He was an impeccable leader. I had reached an age of reckoning. I needed to do something, and it had nothing to do with men. I wondered why more people didn't have these conversations. I was profoundly uncomfortable but deeply grateful. This friend had reminded me in no uncertain terms who I was and who I aspired to be. And, as Robert Frost had pointed out in my earlier life that I loved and left: *I had promises to keep.*

New York at Last

Joe had gone to New York before me. He had been writing me letters. He said he had rented an apartment I was welcome to stay in. Not much room but he and his girlfriend Kari would be glad to have me. I drove the nine hours to Mom's for a few days and made my plane reservations. I had little money, but Mom gave me what she could and somehow it all came together once I had made the commitment to go. This might have been the greatest lesson I learned from my long-time participation in *est*. The nature and power of commitment. I had seen it again and again. I had suffered terrible back trouble in my life. To heal from this pain and annoyance ranked high on every list of goals I made in every seminar I took. I had bouts of fatigue and numbness that baffled me and stopped me in my tracks from my last year in college for many years after that. If it were not for the growing practice of keeping my word and exercising, I might have gone to bed and declared myself disabled. If it weren't for the support, knowledge, love and power of truth-telling, I might have decided to go back home to Missouri and pick up where I left off at Lakeland Restaurant, or some such place. But I went to New York. I stepped off the plane and into a foreign land of dizzying surprises, possibilities, challenges and flops.

Instead of three weeks, the plan to adjust to Kansas City, I gave myself three months.

Of course, I went to the Center. We called it the Center now, not the office. New York Area Center was huge and loud. Phone banks. Desks. Private offices, beyond which were classrooms, conference rooms, copy and fax room. But I was no stranger. I had assisted in California and in Dallas. I knew the ropes, the drill, the game plan. I signed up for a three-month agreement in what was called training management. Phoning, welcoming, making sure everyone had their forms filled out, their goals identified, their deposit and balance arranged.

In my other life I was directed to the Actor's Institute where I enrolled in acting classes. I got a job as a waitress in a restaurant off of Broadway on 72nd St. called Mrs. J's Sacred Cow, where there was a piano bar, and the servers took turns singing. It was glamorous, I thought. But less than a month I got fired. I felt defeated, confused, angry, and lost. "You're a great performer," said the manager, "but you're no waitress." What? I had been waiting tables for about fifteen years. I was proud to be a great server. But the manager at Mrs. J's was telling me something I should have listened to. I was no waitress. Anymore. It was true, I had lost patience with the whole business of taking orders, seeing to it everyone had what they needed, making sure their every need attended to and fulfilled. I had fantasies of pouring coffee on customers' heads, slapping their faces with menus when they couldn't make up their minds. I grew tired of their complaints, their demands, their silly sense of privilege and their pointless conversations. I should have listened, but I kept going, getting fired from two more waitressing jobs. Then I got into computers.

The pay for temp work at night in the city was a whopping $15.00 an hour. I couldn't imagine making this kind of money, but I was determined to do it. I could type like the wind but knew absolutely nothing about computers. I bluffed my way into these fly-by-night jobs. I would go to the big, intimidating and heartless building, go through security, take the elevator up to the 22nd floor and find a computer to sit in front of. I sat glaring at the cold blue light of the screen and practiced acting like I knew what I was doing. Mom always said, "Walk in like you own the joint. Always make them think you know what you're doing." So, I sat there acting like I knew what I was doing, then I would spy someone who looked like they really did know what they were doing. A smart looking young man with glasses. Someone who had a harmless air about them, no problem showing a newbie how to get into the system, then get started on a word processing document. An assignment might last two or three weeks or more. In a few nights I had it down. I worked 11pm-7am. I did it but I don't know how. I didn't do it long, because I wasn't cut out for the late-night shift. I was an early bird, going back to my college days with Carol Sue. But no one knew that, but me. I collected my paycheck and kept my eyes open for other work.

I started with Comptomark, an ad agency on 52nd St. It was quiet, 9-5, and pretty easy. Except for Bob, my boss. He was condescending and inscrutable. All my "be with" training was lost on Bob. He liked to bend over me and say things like, "Three things, Julie. Three things when you arrive: Retrieve the messages, make the coffee, unlock the sliding window for visitors. Just remember: three things. I would have liked to do some other three things when Bob said things like this: Stand up, grab my purse and coat, put up my middle finger, walk out the door. Ok, four things. But of course I said nothing. Nodding, smiling, overlooking, pleasing.

New York at Last

Men, I thought to myself. The older they get, the more insufferable they can be. Bob must have been about fifty.

My first digs in New York were on Ave. B., the lower East Side. It was summer and the livin' was not easy for a lot of folks. Joe had said this was a light-filled apartment in a family section of town. It was loud, dirty, garbage and trash everywhere. The two-bedroom apartment was small, with no air conditioning. Naturally, at night you would want to sleep with the windows open. Not a chance. The heat, the noise and the bugs made you run to shut the window. A fan did little good. I stayed there a few weeks then got a sublet on the Upper East Side. This gal was gone for several weeks, leaving me with her charming but tiny garden apartment on East 84th St. and Lexington. What a difference, like the Beverly Hillbillies before and after moving to L.A. I was able to have coffee in the tiny garden space out her back door. I could look up and see sky, which I needed. It was in that garden apartment I had my epiphany about relationships.

My new, very smart, very cool and clever friend who lived on East 48th St. had a copy of a book called "The Great White Brotherhood." The Great White Brotherhood had nothing to do with race, rather it referred to the white of light that emanates from someone living a life of righteousness and personal power. It was a belief system related to Theosophy and what others knew to be the New Age. Its roots were European, Tibetan, and had swept into America in the late eighteenth century. Christine and I read some of this material, as well as Autobiography of a Yogi and Siddhartha, the story of the Buddha. My mind was stretched and expanded, "curiosified" and occasionally, blown. The one thing I came away with in this intense exploration of spiritual power and possibility (on a very personal level) was that I was wasting energy, precious energy. I didn't look at sexual exploration and activity as sin so much as I saw it as depletion. I never turned against sex, but I cultivated a greater respect for it. I didn't want to abandon it; I wanted to give it its proper place in my life.

And so, I decided this was it. No more casual sex. By casual I meant uncommitted. My energy was something to be valued, not squandered, considered deeply and respected. It was not because I was bad that I made this decision. It was because I had had it with guy after guy and no commitment. No date no ring, as it was sometimes described, meant no future with me.

Okay. I wasn't entirely successful. But I was somewhat successful.

While in the apartment on East 83rd St. and Lex. I met and was "with" a beautiful boy named Leo from New Zealand. It was casual. It was light. You could say it was just what I needed, if it had been ten years earlier. But it wasn't. One night after work, Leo came by and rang the buzzer. We had a brief conversation in which I told him I liked him, but it was over. I didn't want to marry him, and I knew (or was pretty sure) that he didn't want to marry me. It was going nowhere. It was treading water. It was dallying in a playground I had outgrown. Good-bye, Leo, I said. He stood at the door obviously frustrated and a bit confused. Good-bye, I waved, looking into space. He spoke my name a couple of times and then left. I lay there on my couch feeling empty but hopeful. Had I done the right thing? I had definitely done something.

New York, New York. So great they named it twice. That's what they said about it in the song. But that first three months was a killer. I wouldn't go home, although once again, Mom said, "Just come home." A thousand times, I got out of the subway and had to ask, *Which way do I go to 42nd St.?* A thousand times, I closed my eyes tight and held onto the door with a death grip, as my taxi swerved and lurched through endless traffic at any time of day. A thousand people I made my way through grunting, saying excuse me, hurrying in order to be back from lunch after my yoga class in midtown. Somehow, I formed my life around that of a New Yorker, like a heart rock being shaped by the rushing river over a century or so. Only this time it was three months. At the end of three months, I could honestly say over the top of my breathless bewilderment: I loved New York. I loved the insane pace. I loved the challenge of just getting across town. I loved Central Park. I loved the dizzying array of people and cultures, the sounds and sights and smells.

Once Mom came to visit me. She made it all the way from Springfield, Missouri to LaGuardia airport. I met her and we took a taxi back to my place. I could see in Mom's eyes the stars of enchantment that must have been in mine when I first landed and got into town. Everything was different, fast, exciting and wonderful for her. She wanted to try all the foods (loved bagels, hated lobster), see all the sights (Empire State, Wax Museum, riverboat cruises), and just hang around the apartment with me. Mom had stopped drinking and taken the *est* training. She had gone back to church. That didn't ruin her, for which I was grateful. If there's anything I couldn't stand then or now, it was a religious fanatic who judged everyone out there who wasn't so-called "saved." No, Mom was a sweetheart.

We never (as she would say) had a cross word. We were back to being buddies. When I was a teenager, I always used to roll her hair on the weekends. I was sometimes rough, poking her with the picks that were used to keep the brush rollers in place. Ow! She would involuntarily yelp several times after each shampoo. I knew that I was expressing anger with Mom for a number of things. But I never admitted it. I thank God that in later years I rolled her hair with gentleness and precision that she appreciated and remarked on. Oh. And guess where she wanted to go on New Year's Eve when she visited me in New York? Times Square. In the fourteen years I lived in Manhattan, that was the only time I would end up going to that insane, chaotic and delirious show of human hilarity and celebration. The look on Mom's face was ecstatic. She told me if she were a young person, she would move to New York in a minute, a New York City minute. I saw my mom as a young person in that moment. I also saw, with no shadow of darkness, myself in her glowing eyes.

When the woman from whom I had sub-let came back, I stayed with new friends in Chelsea. They were big into Amway. From the Great White Brotherhood to Amway seminars and pre-planned trips to fancy parts of town just to get your juices going for being rich. I went to a couple of these seminars and nearly signed up to be a distributor a time or two. But in the end, I couldn't do it. There was something about the lure of being rich which focused mostly on getting others to join you in your "downline" that didn't square with my spiritual inclinations nor my Ozark upbringing. There was a religious fervor in Amway, it seemed. But there was no center upon which to focus my energy and my devotion. And all that smiling was not my cup of tea. I really liked the so-called "energy bars," but not enough to become a distributor. I truly appreciated the time spent with my friends, not to mention being able to sleep on their couch for a couple of weeks. But Amway was not going to have the pleasure of my allegiance or participation.

At the Actors' Institute, where I took classes and enjoyed community with other "esties" I found an ad for an apartment on West 95th St. It was hand-written on a yellow index card, tacked to a bulletin board:

Julie G. Olmsted

WANTED: ROOMMATE. TWO BEDROOM FIFTH FLOOR APARTMENT, PRE-WAR BUILDING. ELEVATOR. BETWEEN COLUMBUS AVE. AND CENTRAL PARK. $250.00 PER MONTH. CONTACT JOE ROSENTHAL AT THIS NUMBER.

Joe and I were the best of roommates. Total respect. No funny business. Complimentary schedules. Absolute workability. I had the one bathroom to myself in the mornings from 7-7:15. He had it from 7:15-7:30. He was off to work; so was I. I caught the 2 or 3 at 96th and Broadway, then crossed over to the #7 at Penn Station to get to Grand Central. From there to work it was a fifteen-minute walk. In the evenings we were usually assisting or auditioning (me, that is). I had acting classes, seminars, and sometimes, an evening at home. Those were rare opportunities to rest, clean, listen to music and write. I wrote songs and poems and fluff of various sorts. I had some focus but my great desire at this point was to get married. I joked and said I was "so ripe I was falling off the tree." I meant it. I had an urgency to make a life and a family with someone. I made lists of desirable qualities and timelines of intentions. I became more serious about my long-time aspiration of becoming a "happy, well-adjusted human being," I had shared with my classmate Eldon in high school so long ago. Here's a song remnant I wrote at this time of hope and despair.

> *Life at thirty for a small-town girl in a big city office with a pocket full of dreams.*
> *What ever happened to the carefree notions of a woman-child of seventeen?*
> *Remember times. Remember loves. Remember all that summer starlit ecstasy-*
> *Remember locks on the books filled with pretty blue pages,*
> *Full of tales of how it someday all would be.*
> *I'm free. I'm free. Watch me falling, and then flying like a bird.*
> *Look at me. Look at me. Look at how I glide and tumble with a word.*

I messed up plenty. I gained and lost weight. Then gained it back. I quit smoking, then started again, then quit again. I went out with men who were interesting, complicated, unavailable, married. I flirted, got into trouble, then made amends and carried on in my search for "the one." More than once, I cried to my friend Christine, "Wrong, wrong, I must be doing something really, really wrong!" I thought about giving up but that seemed impossible. I had a mission and I'm afraid that it was obvious to some who might otherwise have had a stronger interest in something long-term with me.

Joe moved out to live with his girlfriend a few blocks away and left me with the need to find a roommate. It wasn't hard.

Rick

Ricky was a writer and a comic. I met him in a seminar, and he kept me laughing the entire evening. He could be hilarious, and he could be frightening. For, although he never intimated that we might get married, he was intensely jealous. Once a guy friend called me and Rick heard me say, "What can I do you for?" I had no designs in saying that. It was just silly banter. I thought Rick might kill me. I had never encountered jealousy like this, except maybe with Mom and Daddy Sag. It was totally foreign to me personally. Another time I introduced him to a former boyfriend, then made the mistake of revealing that fact. He almost hit me. I ran outside the apartment and called him an hour or so later to see if he had cooled off enough for me to return. When Ricky was assisting one night, his supervisor asked him if he was going to marry me. He said no. I heard this and ended the relationship. He moved out. And I was "alone again, naturally," as the song said, in the seventies.

Only this wasn't the seventies. This was the eighties. I was over thirty and I had had it (once again) with jerks and wimps and unavailable men. This frustration was right before the peace overtook me. It was like a bubble, or a blister that had burst without fanfare but had provided great relief. I made a plan that I intended to implement. I made it with no attachment and the understanding that things might not work out as I planned them.

Still, I thought, no harm in engaging in the search process. There is something dramatically different about going for something in desperation and setting a goal you understand you may never achieve. The goal is a guide not an imperative. I didn't have to be married. I could do worse than working as a volunteer for a transformative personal development organization and being a sometime actress and legal secretary. That was my job now. I was good at it and had decent steady income. It wasn't a glorious position, but it was better than being a receptionist at the ad agency, moonlighting word processing, or waitressing. Much better. I had settled in as the New Yorker I now was.

Unlikely Help

It was a book that made all the difference. I hesitate to even type the words, but it seems dishonest not to: *How to Marry a Good Man,* by Gail Kessler. This book title is evidence of my seriousness about my goal. The author maintained that women used to be schooled in the art of finding a partner and getting married. No longer. We were all about liberation, equality and self-fulfillment now. It seemed that being happily married kind of got a bad rap back there in the seventies. I was all about those things, too. But, I wondered, did we throw out the baby with the bathwater in some ways? I don't know why meeting someone naturally a few years after high school or college and just waltzing off into the sunset didn't happen for me. I had been married for a couple of months, yes, but that was so long ago, it didn't seem real. I succumbed to that out of frustration, confusion, and a murky sense of self. Maybe all this drama was the result of the seven marriages my parents had between them. But my grandparents had 73 years of marriage to the same person. It wasn't as though I had no examples. Somewhere in between those statistics was me and my dilemma.

Again, I made a promise not to play around with anyone who I could not see myself with in the future. "Three dates" was what my marriage guru had told me. Three dates and you should know if this is something you wish to pursue. If not, have courage. Move on.

I kept working, assisting, auditioning and *intending* in my new, New York life. My new roommate Audrey was also my friend, eventually to become my lifelong best friend. She worked for *est* on staff, so she was gone most of the time. I participated in programs offered at the Actors' Institute, as well as the huge, bustling New York Area Center. I also was almost never home. In Manhattan at the time, the performers' rage was cabaret. In the world of cabaret everything was created, produced, performed and arranged by you. If you could produce the audience, you were a star, for a couple of nights at least. There was always a two-drink minimum plus cover charge, generally five or six dollars. So, as we said, "The more you drink the better we sound." We all had jokes like that. It was a consortium of sorts. We attended each other's shows. We shared tips and lavished compliments, which we secretly hoped would be returned. I tried different voice teachers, believing with all my heart that if I just tried hard enough, I could sound like Linda Ronstadt. It was sometime later that I opened my eyes to the simple fact that singing was a gift not given to everyone. That you couldn't just "try hard" for everything and sooner or later, get it. I got that much. But trying hard was still my modus operandi, in most pursuits. It had worked for me in many ways. In cabaret I cultivated the idea that working hard and developing my "patter" would get me over the hump of a limited singing talent. Patter is the stuff you say between songs. It turned out that I was better at that than singing. A lot better. I loved connecting with people, making them laugh, then counting on their goodness and mercy for my torrid song interpretations. I had a few "really good notes," I used to say. That got me over for a time.

At the Actors' Institute there was a weekend performing workshop modeled after the *est* training. I say that because the head of the institute was a program leader in est before creating his own organization. The weekend was filled with "sharing" and learning, breakthroughs in performance and often in people's lives. It was in this workshop I changed my first name. I thought that there couldn't be a more boring name than Judy Green. I had played around with names for a few years and in the workshop, I decided to go for it. I made an easy switch from Judy to Julie. It suited me. It was simple yet, I thought, melodic. Much easier to say than Judy, or so I thought. I never regretted this little slip over a couple of letters. I've thought of changing it again a few times, but never made the necessary jump that seemed natural and right in that weekend. I "got myself" newly in this experience. I saw that singing chops were not always the thing. Authenticity was the thing. Whether you could sing like Linda or like Frank, it was who you are that gets you over with your audience and in life. Who you are, not the perfection of your performance, was the golden key.

I was shy in the social aspects of the Institute. I rushed to my classes, arriving just in time, never early. I found chatter never as easy as patter. Small talk was not my thing back then. The pressure to say something interesting was always with me and I had not yet learned to accept myself as a basically quiet person. Nor had it occurred to me that being quiet was acceptable, in most situations. It must have been long ago in my "family or origin" I adopted the thought that I had to keep everything going, manage the flow, the tone, and the outcome of a situation. It was all up to me, I thought, without knowing I was thinking it. In *est* this was called "don't know what you don't know." In other words, a blind spot. Discovering that it was okay to be quiet, as well as not be responsible and control every dang thing around me, was one of the biggest, most freeing revelations of my life. It was a handy tool in my pursuit of a lifelong relationship, which I was still committed to, but no longer desperate for.

Last Stop

As a key student, when the performers' workshops were offered, I was there in the supporting role. One of the instructors, Ellie, counted on me and liked me. There was an upcoming workshop in January. I agreed to be there as the key student. I was working at Vogue Magazine downtown as a secretary/proofreader and liked what I did well enough. It was Friday of the day that the workshop began in the evening. I was having a bad day. I didn't want to go to the workshop. I didn't want to be the key student. I was in a mood, a dark mood. Ellie had said something to me the night before which started a growing tidal surge of jealousy and resentment, as it related to another student. I didn't want to say anything about it, but I had to tell Ellie. I'm not feeling well, I said. To which she replied, *What's going on, Julie?* I kind of told her without saying that much. I was pissed but didn't want to say that it was something *she* said that triggered my mood and my sour outlook. "Well, you know, dear. The cream always rises to the top." Hmm, I didn't know that. I had never heard that in fact, despite having grown up around dairy cows. It was food for thought, however. I paused in our conversation. Ok, I said. I had given my word after all. With all my being I didn't want to go. But having been thoroughly schooled in "Word," I re-committed to going.

It was a full class. The room was dark; the stage was lit. I had arrived early, as agreed, and was busy moving chairs around, taking attendance, making sure Ellie had what she needed, making sure everything was in place for a workshop to run smoothly. I was now a logistics person, someone who looked at the space in ways that anticipated anything that could possibly go wrong, then fix that. The space was a bowl, a context that supported the intention and the seamless outcome of a powerful experience for the students. The workshop was called the Mastery. My job was to make sure that everything lived up to that name. I was happy to be invisible as a behind-the-scenes participant. Always in the background or smack in the middle of the stage. Those were my comfort zones.

The night began. Each attendee of the workshop had prepared a song or a monologue. The first meeting was a run-through. No feedback from the instructor, just performance. A deeper experience was in store for all day Saturday. There were about twenty-five participants. The idea of the Mastery was to support aspiring actors and performers to put forth their authentic selves. We were to be vulnerable and courageous, confident and undefended, fierce and connected to our art and our audience. This was the foundation that was set before the first participant stepped onto the stage. Each student had pieces of paper they could use to write words of support and positive feedback to the performer. As the key student, I collected those pieces of paper.

The night was long. When his or her name was called, each one stepped up with a tentative or eager determination. A smile, deep breath, introduction, begin. So many wonderful performers, many seasoned and professional, some terrified, with great charm despite a less than stellar presentation. Then a showstopper.

It was getting late. He stepped onto the stage with his guitar swinging comfortably from his shoulder, crossing his body with ease and familiarity. He wore a green sweatshirt, blue jeans and white sneakers. His dark brown hair was a little long, framing his face with shiny waves. His glasses were an asset, making his handsome face not too handsome to be unapproachable. Then he strummed his guitar powerfully, confidently, a big strum, really out there in its confidence and fierceness. We were all immediately connected, almost breathless. The song was "Be Here Now." I was transfixed, along with everyone else.

You've been hurt by some crazy men
Sorry I couldn't be there then
Let 'em go let me show you how
I want you to be here now

Well, your mama ain't here now
And my mama ain't here now
It's just you and me now.
Be here now

He had written the song, the music, and the lyrics. There was a supportive atmosphere to begin with. But this was an arrow shot through the entire woods into the center of an unseen target. The audience exploded in applause, shouts and whistles. I, as the key student, was subdued. Subdued but rapt. I observed: no wedding ring. The right height. He could have stood up straighter and his feet were a bit pronated. The white sneakers didn't help. But my marriage manual had talked about the "blue plate special." The blue plate special in diners is a special *the way that it is.* There are no substitutions on the special. That's what makes it a special. Many women want to change things around so much that the special is no longer the special and thus, no longer available. As a result, they miss out. Key questions, much more important than most: Would this guy make a good father? Was he a good person? Could he make you laugh? I was about to find out.

Ticket to Ride

A bunch of us piled into a Checker Cab to go uptown and share the fare. Someone suggested we all go get a beer together. "You wanna go for a beer?" I asked my new friend Jeff, who happened to be sitting beside me." "I'm pretty tired. Think I'll just head home tonight." Thinking, thinking. Keep it light. "Well, how about dinner on the break tomorrow night?" "Sounds good." Okay, all right. Easy does it, sounds good to me, too, Bud.

The next day was a long one. When I picked up the little pile of notes to be handed back to students that morning, I found one for me. Hi, Julie! Signed, Jeff-O. Happy face. My heart did a little jig and then I got back "on purpose." No sense in overreacting, just yet. The day progressed slowly, many wonderful performances, lots of great coaching from Ellie. Then, finally, dinner. We walked smoothly and casually toward each other, with our coats and scarves, gloves and hats tumbling over us. Where you want to go? How about Al Buon Gusto? Sounds good. We walked in the light swirling snow toward the restaurant on West 72nd St., all the traffic lights, storefronts and car horns enveloping us. The cold air felt good.

Throughout dinner, I did most of the talking. My apartment. The est Training. My home in Missouri, my experience of the Actor's Institute. Blah, blah, blah. I wasn't sure how I was coming off, but he kept smiling. "I feel wildly self-expressive," I actually said at one point. I didn't know what had come over me. I don't think Jeff did either. It was a nice dinner, but I wondered, what did *he* have to say? I liked talking, but I liked listening, too. I didn't do too much of that this night. I did a lot of looking, however. And I liked what I saw. At one point he disclosed that he had just come out of a relationship and wasn't really over it. Who was this person? I thought to myself. I'll beat her up.

"I seem to have developed a pattern with women I get involved with," he said. "Maybe your pattern is changing," I said cheerily.

"It's with women who are daughters of alcoholics."

"Or maybe it's not," I responded light-heartedly. Jeff and I laughed. Then he picked up the check and we headed back to the workshop.

"How'd you like to go to a Special Guest Seminar with me Monday night?" I asked walking back. Werner Erhard was going to be speaking at Lincoln Center. He was speaking there *in person*. I communicated that this was a very big deal to my new friend. I told him that people usually "spiff up" at these events. I liked jeans and a sweatshirt and white sneakers all right, but I needed to see if this guy knew how to dress up a bit. "Okay," he said. "I'll spiff."

Sunday was the last day of the weekend workshop. I had lots to do and wasn't really available for comment that day. Jeff and I exchanged glances a few times and that was nice. The end of the day came early evening. What did it have in store for me? Nothing, it turned out. I saw Jeff walking out with another girl, woman, actually. An older woman who was a very accomplished singer, songwriter, and guitar player. They walked off together! My heart sank. But I knew I was going to have another chance the next night at the seminar, so I let it go. I was disappointed to see him leave with her, but not too much. I was on a mission and was ready for whatever my next move would be, including nothing. This was a valuable teaching of my book. You are intentional without being desperate. She suggested that if after three times being together, if you saw it going nowhere, gracefully move on. If things are going great and, in a year or so, if you're not engaged, you can actually say something like, "I have the need to be married. I can see this not going in that direction. Best of luck, good-bye." It took character and more than a little discipline to approach relationships this way. Much different than I had in the past. But I trusted my new teacher. And I knew what I wanted. If this wasn't going to be "it," then I would move on. Not happily necessarily, but with some self-respect and integrity.

He showed up looking like the cover of GQ magazine. Grey pin-striped, three-piece suit, blue shirt, red tie. No sneakers. It knocked me off my feet to see him this way. For some reason we stopped by Ellie's apartment on 93rd St. before we went to the event. We chatted with her. She was beaming, and later told me it was because she had introduced us. Wasn't I glad I had decided to keep my word and be her key student? Well yes, I was. He let the fact that he was a Yale grad drop while we were chatting. It was something like, "I went rogue in my family and attended Yale instead of Harvard." Well, Hubba, Hubba, my Ozark self said silently. As we walked downstairs to the street, I quipped, "Yale, huh? I'm impressed." He flashed me a big "be-here-now" kind of smile. He was beautiful, I decided. Green eyes behind nerdy glasses. A generous mouth and strong jaw. Good dad genes. We took the M104 bus down to Columbus Circle and entered the large auditorium, which was full. At the break he registered for the training, which was now called the Forum. He pulled out a checkbook (I had told him to bring) and paid in full. I gulped. He was batting a thousand.

Then out in the lobby he saw someone he knew and introduced me as his friend. I flashed on the night before and the older gal he left with. The lights seemed dimmer in the building. We grabbed a bite to eat then he went his way to 64th St, me uptown to 95th St. No kiss. *No kiss.* Something I definitely was not used to. See you sometime. I'll be at your graduation. Humph. I was not a happy camper. I walked into my apartment, threw my purse across the room, and said to the four walls, "That's it on YOU, buster!"

My brain was scrambled for a couple of days. I had felt a connection. I had seen a possible future. I thought I was onto something good. Now I was unsure. I wanted to move on in my mind, but this was going to take a while, I admitted to myself. I wasn't heartbroken, just a little jammed up. A couple of days passed. Then I walked into the apartment and played my messages. "Hey, Julie. It's Jeff. Uh… I'm a little scared… Anyway, I called to see if you'd like to come to my apartment for dinner on Friday. Let me know. Bye."

He's a little scared? A little scared? That's very good! I exclaimed to the universe, who only wanted my happiness and prosperity. Very good, indeed. I danced around the apartment a bit. Made a sandwich. Played it cool to no one watching. It felt good to be pursued. I twirled. I waited a good, long fifteen-twenty minutes. Then I called to accept the invitation.

He served baked chicken, steamed broccoli and brown rice. His apartment was a small but neat. He was a musician and evidence of that was everywhere. Keyboard, sheet music, boom mic, music stands, fake books. He made a living from music. He wrote charts, lead sheets, accompanied singers, played for classes like the mastery. He was the musician for a puppet theater group in the City called the Shadow Box Theater. He liked to talk about philosophy, knew a lot about religion and was fascinated with cults and group dynamics. He had done something a lot like *est* and was looking forward to the Forum. He was funny and laughed at my jokes, too. Being together with Jeff that night was like homecoming. It was natural and light. We finished dinner, stood up to clear the table and I took a breath, "Do you think you'll ever kiss me?" "Uh, well, yes, of course, you know." We embraced and the spell was cast. I don't think we were apart for much more than a day or two after that.

He taught me about many things. Theater. Songwriting. Cheese Danish. A Course in Miracles. Massachusetts. Coffee Yoga, (pour-over coffee in a Melitta coffee carafe). Swiss Mocha Almond from the fancy *Alpine* deli down the street. We listened to music, wrote music, sang together and sat in silence with comfy ease. We wrote a song based on a line that came to me while picking up breakfast at the deli, *How good can you stand it?* Here's the chorus:

How good can you stand it?
The choice is yours to make.
How good can you stand it?
How much love can you take?

One night we made chimichangas and had too much to drink. We were so full of chimichangas and drunk from the margaritas, we crawled across his apartment, laughing and moaning till we fell asleep.

We wrote, created, and starred in many cabaret shows.

Jeff and "Jewel" Early Days in NYC Shadow Box Theatre

He got me an audition at the Shadow Box Theater. I was easily hired, which meant that now we were together both night and day.

Once while hanging out in his apartment, he was working, and I was writing. I wondered to myself then asked, "Do you ever get angry?" He looked up from the chart he was working on and said with great seriousness, "Yes. I do." "Good," was all I said. It was important to me to be with someone who had limits, boundaries, stuff up with which he would not put. I needed that. I knew myself that well.

After lovemaking one night, we were all tangled up together and he said as if he were surprised to realize it, "You're everything I've been looking for." I smiled in the darkness then replied softly, "Yep. Here I am. In living color.

He moved into my apartment on West 95th St. We worked together, rode the bus together, ate, drank and laughed together. We took seminars in what was at this point called the Forum. In seminars we always had homework. He was sitting at the window of our humble 95th St. apartment one sunny day in May. The homework was to compile a list of "withholds, undelivered communications and incompletions." I was lazily reading a book on the day bed against the wall. He suddenly pushed the chair back, stood up and came over to me. He bent down on one knee. I turned my head to him in amused curiosity. "I have an undelivered communication," he said. "Yes?" My heart sped up a bit.

Day of Engagement

"Will you marry me?"

I gulped, smiled, and said, "Let me think about it (1…2…) Yes. I will."

Julie G. Olmsted

I jumped up and down for a while, then we got on the phone, calling everyone we knew. We set a date, four months from the day, October 25. I was spinning with happiness and rooted in certainty, a strange and unfamiliar feeling for me. This was the place I knew I belonged. And it wasn't a place at all. It was a person. And I felt I was finally home. Here in New York City, on the Upper West Side, with a musical genius who went to Yale. Go figure. I was impressed with my hillbilly self.

Here is the song we wrote that was sung at our New York City wedding, in the penthouse home of the director of The Shadow Box Theater where we worked.

Coming Home
When I look into your eyes,
Somehow, I can recognize
Loving you is coming home to me.
Touch me, I become a star, heaven's right here where you are.
It's coming home to you that set me free.

Somehow it feels so familiar, tho' I can't believe what I'm seeing. I seem to remember agreeing to meet you right here, right now.

A thousand years will melt away, they couldn't mean more than today, my search has ended, and I'm coming home to you…

Afterword

Once my dear friend Diana expressed concern about her sister hanging out with me. She said something like, "You're a hip woman of the seventies and I'm just not sure that is a good thing for her." Why hip? I was confused but compelled, adventurous but bumbling. In love with the world but desperate for something deeper. Did this make me hip? I went to college and had *ideas* about life. I had a lot of boyfriends. I lived on my own and drove all over God's creation. I know my hometown friends never went far from the cradle of their childhoods. That wasn't for me. I had a call, a silent bell ringing in my soul. I had to be about some business I didn't know the source or nature of.

I end this narrative of brokenness, chaos and adventure with having found my partner in life. A steadfast partner of over forty years now. Does that mean that all roads led to him? No more than at any point of life where one might look back and notice that things were never the same after. I simply see myself entering a new era when we met and married, an era worth remembering but different and so much calmer than previous ones. I believe the struggles, wrong turns and detours I took were part of a longing for something. And that something was the formation of the core of myself, independent of the imitation of others, free, in part at least, from the patterns of the past. The formation of something there but only detected, not seen or known. In each and every leaving, there was sorrow. In each and every beginning there was struggle. To adjust. To see clearly. To find the four candles in the Christian Advent wreath: *Hope, Peace, Joy and Love.*

The point of a thousand stories (from Genesis in the Bible to movies of the day) is that all of us want to share our lives with someone. It could be someone for a little while. It could be someone for the rest of our days. In my case, I do believe that I found my partner coming from a place of wholeness, not desperation. That for me was the golden key.

All along the way, my faith in goodness has buoyed me up. My friends, my longing, my love of the beauty of this life, and my willingness to go through whatever I needed to (eventually, if not immediately) all helped me to anchor myself in the rest of my life, coming around to a place just right, without the need to move from one town, one person, one situation and one passion to the next. I have refrained from laying on myself a diagnosis or a condition that pigeonholes my characteristics, or limits my ideas of who I am.

I do now know that this longing is universal. I do now know that some are meant to wander, if not geographically, then through learning, not knowing, and inner exploring; there are countless songs, poems and themes in art and story demonstrating this. I am the product of the times and the circumstances of my birth. And I am myself, untouched by any outside person or thing. The Rumi poem *Love Dogs* addresses some of this longing:

This longing you express is the return message. The grief you cry out from draws you toward union. Your pure sadness that wants help is the secret cup.

My pure sadness has never been too far from me.

There are love dogs no one knows the name of. Give your life to be one of them.

Imagine. Give your life to be a love dog. It works for me.

There is the psychological model in which to hold your life. There is the spiritual model. I salute the former. I embrace the latter.

I have come to believe that in heaven, our true home that we long for, and that reflects our true nature, there is the sweetness and goodness of the love God intends. We may have to work and search for it, but it is for everyone who seeks it. In every sunrise, I can see it. In every starry night, it calls out.

Cheers. A round of cornbread and honey butter for the house.

Acknowledgments

I thank my publisher Stephanie Larkin for her enthusiasm and support.

I thank Robin and Carol and my writing group for their encouragement and guidance.

All my mentors and the kind and loving adults who told me to keep going and never give up on myself and my life.

Thanks and love to Audrey, Christine and Dee for believing in my writing.

I thank my husband for hearing me, correcting me and loving me through any and everything.

I thank God for the patience and grace I've been shown whenever I have been willing to be open to a miracle, no matter the letting go that might have preceded it.

I thank Werner Erhard for the gift of transformation that never leaves me.

I thank my dear mother and grannie, who live in and through me in the ways of goodness and mercy always.

www.ingramcontent.com/pod-product-compliance
Lightning Source LLC
Chambersburg PA
CBHW060609080526
44585CB00013B/755